THE MORO AFFAIR

LEONARDO SCIASCIA was born in Sicily in 1912. He was a renowned Italian novelist and essayist, as well as a polemical and outspoken political commentator who, like many of the protagonists in his novels, challenged the entrenched corruption in the government of his day. He has been described by Gore Vidal as one of the greatest modern writers. He died in 1989.

*Also by Leonardo Sciascia and
available from Granta Books*

The Wine-Dark Sea
The Day of the Owl
Sicilian Uncles
Equal Danger
The Knight and Death *and* One Way or Another

THE MORO AFFAIR

Leonardo Sciascia

Translated from the Italian by

SACHA RABINOVITCH

Foreword by

NEIL BELTON

GRANTA

Granta Publications, 12 Addison Avenue, London W11 4QR

Published in Great Britain by Granta Books 2002
This edition published by Granta Books 2013
First published in Great Britain by Carcanet Press Ltd 1987
First published in Italy as *L'Affaire Moro* 1978

A CIP catalogue record for this book
is available from the British Library.

13 5 7 9 10 8 6 4 2

ISBN 978 1 84708 929 8

Printed and bound by CPI Group (UK) Ltd, Croydon, CR0 4YY

FOREWORD

The Background to *The Moro Affair*.

Aldo Moro was known as 'the master weaver' of Italian politics, a subtle manipulator of power. Prime Minister on five occasions, and President of the Christian Democratic Party at the time of his death, he ended helplessly and horribly. He was kidnapped in March 1978 and held for fifty-four days by a small group of Leninist guerillas, who then shot him and dumped his body in the back of a car on a Roman street. The culture that produced him, the reluctance of his friends to work for his release, the unexplained lapses in police work and the implications of his death, form the subject of Leonardo Sciascia's dense and passionate book.

For over thirty years Moro was a dominant figure in a one-party state. Its citizens enjoyed freedom of the press and of assembly, and a fair number of personal liberties. They could also participate in democratic elections, as long as these elections had only one outcome: victory for the Christian Democrats, who dominated every postwar government until the end of the Cold War. The major opposition grouping, the Italian Communist Party, could never be brought into government, even as a junior partner.

Cold War rules were simple but strict. Washington would not allow a party owing even residual allegiance to Moscow to govern a Western country. This was the reality of power. The communists accepted the parliamentary system and ran the regions they controlled very well, making Emilia-Romagna a model of local government, but in the geo-political terms that mattered during the Cold War they remained beyond the pale. The Christian Democrats usually governed in a coalition with one or two of the smaller right-wing parties, and later the non-communist socialists.

The absence of a legitimate opposition locked a bizarre system into place, with a vibrant economy and culture and a society corrupt and immobile when it came to reforming even obvious abuses. Government jobs were a political matter, as were contracts and development grants. The Mafia flourished in the south, often with the permission of the Christian Democratic establishment. The smallest effort to make the country more efficient, accountable and democratic – like rationalizing the building boom that was disfiguring Italian cities – got stuck in the mud of bureaucratic delay. There was no sense of the state as an institution that should be made to work on behalf of its citizens. Hence Sciascia's caustic irony at Christian Democracy's sudden discovery of state integrity – the party refused to negotiate over Moro's release, despite his increasingly desperate appeals from his 'people's prison'.

The princes of this weird republic were the chiefs of the Christian Democrat factions, men like Moro who disposed of patronage through their networks of parliamentary deputies, city politicians, businessmen and activists. Aldo Moro was, within the numbing limitations of Italian politics, a brilliant tactician. He succeeded in bringing the PSI, the socialists once hostile to both Moscow and Washington, into a coalition government between 1963 and 1966. The party was neutralized, corrupted and split, and no longer available for alliance with the communists. When he was kidnapped, Moro was on his way to 'consecrate' (his word) an agreement whereby the communists would support the government in the face of a national crisis. Forces on the right as well as the left were not happy with this arrangement, known as the 'historic compromise'. But the communist leader Enrico Berlinguer was determined to prevent an Italian version of the Chilean disaster of 1973, when a government of the left unleashed an upsurge of demands by the poor and ran into a wall of panic and resistance put up by the elites and the armed forces. The result was Pinochet's coup.

By 1978 the enormous social and technological changes of the previous twenty years had turned Italy into an unstable mess. The frustrations of poor peasants, Fiat production workers, small shopkeepers outraged by long hair and pornography, women seeking the right to divorce and students anxious about jobs could no longer be managed within the old system. Strikes and protests led to street violence, occupations, situationist gestures and even outright insurrection. The student left did not settle down after 1968, as it did in other countries, but turned to extreme versions of Leninist politics and talked of armed uprising. Some of these young people took their own rhetoric very seriously. They began beating, and later shooting, managers, foremen and journalists who they accused of oppression. The Red Brigades were a tiny faction, never more than a few dozen strong, but they transformed an argument over reform into a hysterical debate about law and order. Their effect on Italian politics was disastrous.

The state bureaucracy and the armed services, meanwhile, were full of right-wingers who regarded democracy as a bad alternative to Mussolini's fascism. There were a couple of farcical attempted coups. Bombings attributed to anarchists later turned out to be the work of neo-fascists protected by the security services. These were years in which paranoid conspiracy theories were the subject of everyday conversation in Italy, and often referred to something real.

When the Red Brigades seized Moro and killed his five bodyguards, their continued existence was a surprise to most Italians. In 1976, they seemed to have been mopped up by the police. The mysteriously renewed efficiency of this ultra-left band gives Sciascia pause for thought. In Italy nothing works, yet 'the Red Brigades function to perfection'. In this respect, he reflects, they are like the Mafia, about which Sciascia knew a lot. He suggests that the real function of the Red Brigades, mad as they are, might be to shift power around the places where it already resides. (He had already explored this theme in his novel *Equal Danger*, published in 1971.)

Sciascia wrote this book in the summer of 1978. In 1979 he became a parliamentary deputy, on the list of the tiny Radical Party. In his minority report to the Parliamentary Commission of Inquiry on the Moro affair, issued in June 1982 and included in this volume, he is scathing about the failures of the police in their search for Moro. In Rome they swamped the city with 4,000 policemen carrying out searches and roadblocks; on the day of the murders they were stopping cars in villages in Sicily, hundreds of miles from the scene of the crime. Yet they could not spare a dozen men to tail a key suspect who might have led them to the Red Brigades' hideout. Nor did they analyse Moro's letters – which his captors made public in order to sow dissent among the mainstream parties – for clues to his whereabouts. Sciascia shows how they might have been read more carefully.

The Moro Affair is very much concerned with language. The whole system was drenched in a rhetoric that gave Italian political prose a horrible, ornate quality of dishonesty and meaningless incantation. The communists had their own baroque ways of saying nothing: their daily paper was a byword for sonorous gobbledegook. Moro himself was good at making long soporific speeches full of deliberate ambiguities. Sciascia agrees with Pier Paolo Pasolini that the Church got rid of Latin in its services only for Moro to replace it with a new and equally incomprehensible dead language. Amidst this verbal fog, full of references to renewal and modernization Moro practiced always 'the art of making every innovation serve old purposes'.

The pathos of Moro's letters lies in the disintegration of this 'language of non-expression', and his growing anger at the knowledge that he is being abandoned by people he thought were his friends. A group of eminent associates declared publicly that the man appealing for his life was not the man they knew, implying that he was mad or forced to write as he did. Moro was baffled at their betrayal of the iron law of Christian Democratic solidarity in the face of threats from its enemies – a solidarity that had protected even the most corrupt politicians from legal retribution. Moro's final demand is that when he is buried he should not be 'surrounded by those in power', and Sciascia recognises the importance of this use of the unadorned and normally unspeakable word: 'finally here for the first time he writes the word "power" in all its terrible simplicity – a word he sees at last in all its true, profound and corrupt reality.'

In the twentieth century, writers such as Pound, Junger, Céline, Ehrenburg, Brecht and Sartre became politically engaged, and were tainted by the experience. Sciascia kept his head. His work was an attempt to grapple aesthetically and morally with the human consequences of under-development, organised crime and the dangerous power of ideas. *The Moro Affair* remains an exemplary book by a writer in politics.

Neil Belton

THE MORO AFFAIR

The most monstrous thing to say: that someone has died
'at the just moment'.
— E. Canetti, *The Human Province*

Chronology of the Affair

March 1978

16 Aldo Moro, President of the National Council of Christian
Democrats, is kidnapped, his escort of five men is murdered —
presumably by the Red Brigades. Before nightfall the Government, presided over by Deputy Andreotti, which until then had
been viewed with certain doubts and reservations by some
factions of the Christian Democrats as well as by the left, is
approved in both the Chamber of Deputies and the Senate, by a
majority which includes even the Communists.
One of the cars used by the terrorists is found by the police in via
Lucinio Calvo, about a hundred metres from via Fani where the
kidnapping occurred.

17 A young clerk is arrested, suspected of being involved in
Moro's abduction. However, the magistrate in charge of the
inquest releases him two days later as uninvolved in *the event*. (It
should be noted that the police committed here an outrageous
blunder in promptly arresting a person suspected of such a
crime as abduction, when he should have been shadowed and
watched.)
Another of the cars used by the terrorists is found in via Lucinio
Calvo: was it already there or was it conveyed there later? Since
this is a carefully combed and highly guarded zone, the discovery highlights the inefficiency of the police (and the Red
Brigades' desire to stress it).

18 The Red Brigades' first communiqué is received. They assume
full responsibility for Moro's abduction and for the escort's
murder; they declare their intention of putting the President of
the Christian Democratic Party on trial (*People's Court of*

Justice). A photograph of Moro as prisoner in the 'People's Prison' is enclosed.

19 The third car used for the abduction is found by the police in via Lucinio Calvo. But the possibility of its having been conveyed there later, eluding the guards and patrols, is as alarming as the possibility of its having been there unnoticed for two consecutive days. Nor is this the only mishap the police encounters: among the 'wanted' men whose photographs are broadcast on television and in the papers two are already in custody and one is officially in Paris. Even Brunilde Pertramer, sought as a member of the Red Brigades, turns out to have been regularly registered in the hotels where she has stayed.

20 At the trial of Curcio and others which is proceeding tempestuously at the Turin Law Courts, the caged Red Brigades shout: 'Moro is in our hands!'

21 The Council of Ministers passes an act to increase the power of the police and reduce that of the citizens. The papers consider the advisability of self-censorship and are willing to put it into effect. They invite prominent personalities to pronounce themselves for or against it. Vito Ciancimino, former Mayor of Palermo, when questioned by the *Giornale di Sicilia*, replies: 'As a matter of principle it is a duty to inform the public. But in special circumstances such as those we are undergoing, it may be wiser not to publish the Red Brigades' messages, were it only to assist the investigations. When publication can hinder the progress of investigations and thus the eventual capture of the murderers, silence should be maintained at whatever cost. I repeat that, on principle, freedom of the press should be assured.'

24 In Turin the Red Brigades attack Giovanni Picco, a Christian Democrat and former Mayor of that city.

25 The Red Brigades' second communiqué. It includes a provisional list of charges against Moro.

29 Arrigo Levi, Editor-in-Chief of the Turin daily *La Stampa*, calls for the resignation of President of the Republic Leone and the election by Parliament of Moro in his place. The proposal provokes widespread perplexity and suspicion.

In the evening a letter from Moro together with the Red Brigades' third communiqué reach Francesco Cossiga, Minister of the Interior. The communiqué announces that the trial 'is proceeding with the prisoner's total collaboration'.

31 *L'Osservatore Romano* states the Holy See's willingness to take steps towards a solution of this 'most painful occurrence'.

April

1 It's rumoured that Nicola Rana, Moro's secretary, has received a letter from the prisoner. The next day it's said the family has also received a letter.

3 The police carry out house-to-house searches and arrests among members of the extreme left. But within forty-eight hours the Magistrates release nearly all those arrested — since the police operations were based on lists compiled in 1968. Many of those who were then rebels are members of parties now included in the 'constitutional arch' and especially of the Communist Party.

4 Zaccagnini receives letter from Moro together with the Red Brigades' fourth communiqué and the pamphlet *Risoluzione della Direzione Strategica* dated February 1978. The communiqué declares that 'the stratagems employed by the official press' to suggest that Moro's letter to Cossiga was written under the Red Brigades' dictation 'are as treacherous as they are stupid' since the letter expresses a point of view the Red Brigades don't share.

5 *Il Giorno* publishes a letter from Eleonora Moro to the Editor written in the hope that the Red Brigades will show it to her husband.

7 In Genoa the Red Brigades shoot at Felice Schiavetti, Chairman of *Associazione Industriale*, laming him as is their custom.

10 The papers publish the totally groundless news that the Red Brigades require, in exchange for Moro, President Leone's resignation and sixty-thousand-million lire. In the afternoon the Red Brigades publish their fifth communiqué and an autographed attack by Moro on Taviani.

11 In Turin three members of the Red Brigades shoot the prison warden Lorenzo Cotugno. Before dying, Cotugno wounds

Cristoforo Piancone of the Red Brigades, who is left by his comrades on the doorstep of a hospital. Piancone claims he's a political prisoner and refuses to answer when questioned by the police or the judge. But some days later the dailies *Il Tempo* and *Il Giornale* publish an interview a reporter has managed to obtain from him.

12 It's said that Cossiga, Rana and the Moro family have received letters from Moro.

15 The Red Brigades' sixth communiqué: 'Aldo Moro has been found guilty and has been condemned to death.' The papers announce 'eleven shootings in Venice in seventeen days', up to the previous day; and, cautiously, that a list of two hundred suspected members of the Red Brigades 'appears to have been delivered to the Ministry of the Interior by an eminent representative of the Communist Party.'

17 Appeals to the Red Brigades by the *Osservatore Romano* and Amnesty International.

18 The Red Brigades' 'false' seventh communiqué. The police discover a Red Brigade 'lair' in via Gradoli. By chance, rumour first has it. However it later transpires that the information had been available for some time. Only the police had gone to Gradoli in the province of Viterbo instead of to via Gradoli which is in the district of Rome where Moro was kidnapped.

19 *Lotta Continua*, an extreme left paper, publishes an appeal for Moro's life signed by Bishops, Members of Parliament and both Roman Catholic and lay intellectuals.

20 In Milan the Red Brigades shoot a prison warden, Senior Warrant Officer Franceso De Cataldo.
The Red Brigades publish the 'real' seventh communiqué: Moro is alive and they are ready to exchange him for 'Communist prisoners'. This is an ultimatum. Deadline the 22nd at 3 p.m. A photograph of Moro holding the previous day's *La Republica* is delivered to the above paper.

21 Another letter from Moro to Zaccagnini. Not all the papers publish it.

22 At the University of Padua, Professor Ezio Riondato is shot

four times in the legs by the *Nucleo Combattenti per il Communismo*. Paul VI writes to the 'men of the Red Brigades'.

24 Eighth Red Brigades' communiqué. They demand in exchange for Moro the liberation of thirteen 'Communist prisoners' whom they name.
The Panamanian Government declares that it is willing to receive the terrorists if the Italian Government decides to accept the exchange.
A further letter from Moro to Zaccagnini is delivered to the daily *Vita*.

25 Kurt Waldheim, General Secretary of the UN addresses, through Italian television and speaking in Italian, an appeal to the Red Brigades. It's badly received in Italian political circles — he's accused of having suggested that the terrorists have a 'motive' and therefore an ideal. But it turns out that what Waldheim meant was 'designs' — a slight error of translation.
The following declaration by 'the friends of Moro' is communicated to the press from the Christian Democratic Party's headquarters: 'He is no longer the man we knew.'

26 Ten pistol shots fired at the Christian Democrat Girolamo Mechelli, former Chairman of Regione Lazio. In the legs.
Il Giorno publishes a letter to Moro from his children.

27 In Turin, Sergio Palmieri, head of the Department of Occupational Studies at Mirafiori, is shot in the legs — the Red Brigades claim responsibility in a message received the same day.
Craxi suggests that the State should express its willingness to accept the Red Brigades' terms by showing clemency towards its political prisoners.

28 Andreotti on television: 'How would the Carabinieri, the police and the prison guards respond to the Government's negotiating — behind their backs and in violation of the law — with those who have made havoc of that law? And what would the wives, orphans and mothers of those who have fallen while accomplishing their duty have to say?' Obviously nothing can be done for Moro — like Cortez, Andreotti by referring to mothers, widows and orphans has burnt his boats and made any dealings with the Red Brigades envisaged by Craxi impossible.

29   There is talk of other letters from Moro to his family. And of one delivered by post in reply to that from his children published by *Il Giorno*.

That evening *Il Messagero* receives a letter addressed to the Christian Democratic Party. This is the last of the letters known to us which is addressed to the Party as a whole.

30   It's reported that Moro has sent letters to Leone, Andreotti, Ingrao, Fanfani, Misasi, Piccoli and Craxi. But only those to Craxi and Leone are published, on the 3rd and 4th of May respectively.

May

1   The Moro family appeals to the Christian Democratic Party leaders to 'courageously assume their personal responsibilities'.

3   Andreotti confirms the Government's refusal to negotiate with the Red Brigades.

4   Two lamings: in Milan, Umberto degli Innocenti, of the Sit-Siemens Company; in Genoa, Alfredo Lamberti, of the Italsider factory of Cornigliano.

5   The Red Brigades' ninth communiqué: 'We conclude the battle started on March the 16th with the executing of the sentence to which Aldo Moro was condemned.' Interpretations of the gerundive are launched.

6   In Novara the laming of Giorgio Rossanigo, the prison doctor — this time by the *Proletari Armati per il communismo*.

8   Another doctor, Diego Fava — of the National Institute for Insurance against Illness — is lamed in Milan — once again by the *Proletari Armati per il communismo*.

9   Aldo Moro's body is found in the boot of a Renault — red according to the member of the Red Brigades who gave the information, purple according to the papers.

The family circulates this message: 'The family wish that Aldo Moro's precise instructions should be observed by the State authorities and the Party. That is: no national mourning, State funeral or memorial medals. The family retreats into silence and requires silence. As to Aldo Moro's life and his death, let history judge.'

10   Private funeral at Torrita Tiberina. Moro is buried in the local cemetery.

13   Funeral ceremony at the Basilica of San Giovani in Laterano. Paul VI presides, Cardinal Poletti (who Moro had hoped, without much conviction, might correct the 'blunder') celebrates. Members of the Government are all present. Moro's wife and children are absent. The Pope says: 'Oh Lord, You have not answered our prayers.'

Out for a stroll last night, I saw a glow-worm in the cracked plaster of a wall. I hadn't seen a glow-worm in these parts for at least forty years. That's why I took it first for a fragment of schist or a splinter of glass in the plaster and that it was the moonlight threading through the branches which made it glimmer greenly. The idea that glow-worms had come back after all those years didn't occur to me. They were no more than a memory — from an age when little things were important and provided entertainment and ecstasy. We used to call them *cannileddi di pecuraru* — that's what the country folk called them. A shepherd's life was so miserable with nights spent watching over the flocks, that it seemed only fair he should have the glow-worm as a relic or a reminder of the light, during the awesome dark. Awesome on account of the frequent cattle-raids. Awesome too because it was mainly children who were entrusted with the task of guarding the sheep. Thus 'the little candles of the shepherd'. And from time to time we would catch one, keeping it delicately cupped in our closed fist so as to suddenly reveal that emerald phosphorescence to our younger playmates.

But it was really a glow-worm on that wall. I experienced an intense pleasure. A double pleasure. Somehow reduplicated. The pleasure of rediscovering a time — my childhood, its memories, this very spot, silent now, echoing then with voices and games — and the pleasure of a time to discover, to invent. With Pasolini. For Pasolini. Pasolini who was now outside time but not yet, in this terrible land which Italy has become, transformed into himself ('Tel qu'en lui-même enfin l'éternité le change'). Brotherly and remote Pasolini was to me. A brotherliness without familiarity, guarded and, I think, full of mutual intolerances. There was a word which created for me a sort of barrier between us, a word he loved, a key-word to his life, the word 'adorable'. I may perhaps have written that word at one time or another and I've certainly thought it sometimes — but of a single woman and a single writer. The writer, needless to say, is

Stendhal. But Pasolini found 'adorable' all that for me was already distressing about Italy (and even for him, since I recall his 'adorable because it is distressing' applied to the *Lettere luterane* — and how can one adore what distresses?) and was to become terrible. He found 'adorable' those who were inevitably to be instrumental in his death. And one could compile a small dictionary of the things he described as adorable in his writings and which for me were then simply distressing and are now terrible.

But the glow-worms. And all of a sudden — with compassion and hope — I'm writing for the benefit of Pasolini, as though to resume a correspondence of more than twenty years: 'The glow-worms you thought were extinct are now beginning to re-emerge. I saw one last night after so many years. And it's the same with the crickets: for four or five years I hadn't heard a cricket and now our nights endlessly overflow with their chirping.'

Glow-worms. Government House. Pasolini wanted to prosecute Government House more or less on account of the glow-worms. Of the extinction of glow-worms. 'Since I'm a writer and I write polemically or at least polemicise with other writers, let me give a poetico-literary definition of the phenomenon which occurred in Italy about ten years ago. This will help to clarify and sum up what I have to say (and perhaps make it more easily accessible). In the early 1960s, owing to the pollution of the atmosphere, and especially in the countryside because of the pollution of our waterways (the blue rivers and limpid springs), glow-worms began to vanish. The phenomenon was sudden and devastating. In a couple of years there were no more glow-worms. (They are now a rather distressing relic of our past: an old man who recalls them can't recognize in the boys of today the boy he was, can't have the pleasant regrets he once would have had.)

'Thus I shall call that phenomenon which occurred about ten years ago "the extinction of the glow-worm".

'The Christian Democratic regime had two distinct phases that not only can't be compared to each other — which would imply a certain continuity — but which have become historically incommensurable.

'The first phase of this regime (as the radicals have always rightly insisted on calling it) goes from the end of the war to the extinction of the glow-worm. The second goes from the extinction of the glow-worm up to the present.'

And again: 'In the period of transition — during the extinction of the glow-worm — the Christian Democrat leaders suddenly changed their idiom, adopted a radically new language (as incomprehensible as Latin, too). And Aldo Moro in particular — that is (by an enigmatic correlation) the man who seems to be the least implicated of all in the terrible things which have been perpetrated between 1969 and today, in the endeavour, till now apparently successful, to maintain power at all costs.'

Glow-worms. Government House. The prosecution of Government House. It's as though inside Government House, three years after Pasolini published that article in the *Corriere della sera*, only Aldo Moro still circulated — in those empty rooms, those already abandoned rooms. Abandoned for the sake of other, safer rooms — in a new and vaster House. Safer, obviously, for the guiltiest. 'The least implicated of all' therefore, lagging behind and alone precisely because he was the 'least implicated of all'. And precisely because he was the 'least implicated of all' doomed to a more enigmatic and tragic correlation.

Before this article (published in the *Corriere* of February 1975 as 'The power vacuum in Italy' and later collected in *Scritti corsari* under the title by which it had come to be known, 'The glow-worm article'), Pasolini had written about Moro's idiom in articles and essays on linguistics (and in his book *Empirismo eretico*). But here in the glow-worm piece his interest in Moro, in Moro's language, emerges in a more considered and precise context within a broader and more desperate vision of Italian affairs.

'As usual,' says Pasolini, 'the only symptoms we had were in the language.' Symptoms that the Christian Democratic Government which, ten years ago had been neither more nor less than a survival of Fascism, was heading for a vacuum. In Moro's language — a language that was totally new and yet, on account of its incomprehensibility, able to fill the space from which, precisely in those years, the Roman Catholic Church had removed its Latin. It could almost be seen as an exchange, a substitution. But then, tautologically, Latin is incomprehensible to those who don't know Latin. Pasolini can't make sense of Moro's Latin, that 'totally new language'. But he feels within that incomprehensibility, within that vacuum where it is enunciated and resounds, an 'enigmatic correlation' between Moro and *the others*, between the Moro who ought to have been the last to seek and try out a new Latin (still that 'latinorum' which makes Renzo Tramaglino tremble with impatience) and those who, on the contrary, must — in order to survive were it only as robots, as masks — wallow in it. 'By an enigmatic correlation'. Pasolini's brief, incisive definition seems to predict, to anticipate the Moro affair. Today we know that the 'correlation' was an 'opposition'. And Moro paid for it with his life. but before they murdered him he was compelled, he compelled himself, to endure for nearly two months a terrible requital. For his 'totally new language', for his new Latin which was as incomprehensible as the old. An exact requital. He was obliged to *express* himself in a

18

language of *non-expression*, to *make himself understood* by the same means he had sought and tested in order *not to be understood*. He had to communicate through the language of non-communication. Out of necessity. That is through censorship and self-censorship. As a prisoner. As a spy in enemy territory and under enemy supervision.

But before discussing the *documents of requital*, that is the letters through which Moro endeavoured to communicate with *the others* whom he believed to be 'his men' (for wasn't it he who had invented that totally new language — alibi or disguise — for them?) we must discuss the enemy, the jailers. And in particular we must acknowledge the specific ethics of this enemy, of these jailers, an ethic that could be defined as a jailer's ethic — derived from a direct or second-hand knowledge of Foucault and his followers (although more rough and ready instances of such ethics or attitudes have been seen in the Southern underworld, whether political or not). Sons, grandsons or great-grandsons of Stalinist Communism, the members of the Red Brigades had none the less been subjected to the doctrine of 'investigate and punish' and incorporated this tenuous thread of liberalism into their fossilized ideology. Thanks to this doctrine their prison wasn't intended to copy the prison run by the *Imperialist State of Multinationals* — known as the SIM (Stato Imperialista delle Multinazionali). And a treatise could be written on the proliferation of such abbreviations in the *Risoluzione della direzione strategica delle Brigate rosse*. Their investigations were not intended to achieve the demoralizing, annihilating results experienced by the less stalwart or less indoctrinated prisoners of the SIM jails. A long paragraph in the *Risoluzione* concerns the 're-structuring of prisons' in Italy. As if anything could possibly be restructured in Italy, and as if there was anything new in the fact that a prison's purpose was to annihilate the political prisoner's political identity by means of his physical disintegration. Silvio Pellico and Luigi Settembrini wrote in a very similar vein to that of paragraph D of the Red Brigades' *Risoluzione*.

Members of the Red Brigades, recently prosecuted by the Turin Law Courts, claimed — as proof of their humane attitude towards their prisoners, of their distinctiveness — that Judge Sossi incarcerated in their 'People's Prison' was treated to risotto. Such a gastronomic, homely, intimate note might seem dissonant, almost absurd in that criminal context. But it isn't. Indeed it helps to explain some of the Red Brigades' incongruences, their sometimes disconcerting behaviour in the Moro affair. And especially what might be called their 'postal zeal' insofar as it was excessive and, from a given date, excessively respectful of privacy. By delivering in the course of the affair, and not without risk, between fifty and sixty (the minimum and maximum according to those published) letters from Moro, the Brigades not only kept their material resources needlessly active and on the alert, but furthermore are said to have made a particular point of scrupulously observing the constitutional law concerning postal privacy, the inviolability of the correspondence between free citizens of a free country. From a given date, as we noted. For in their third communiqué, which accompanied Moro's first letter from the 'People's Prison' (the letter addressed to Franceso Cossiga, Minister of the Interior), the Red Brigades had stated a different principle: '[Moro] asked to write a private letter (secret manoeuvres are the norm within the Christian Democratic Mafia) to the Government and more precisely to the Chief Copper Cossiga. His request was granted, but since nothing should be hidden from the people according to our custom, we are making it public.' This principle, forcefully asserted on 29 March, was tacitly overruled on 30 April — the day it became known that letters from Moro had been delivered to Leone, Andreotti, Ingrao, Fanfani, Masasi, Piccoli and Craxi. Of these seven letters, the first was published at Moro's request (he had addressed it to the Press 'with the urgent request to kindly forward it to its distinguished addressee'), as well as that addressed to Craxi who conformed at the time to the position adopted by the PSI (Italian Socialist Party). However those who preferred not to make the contents of their letters known were free to do as they pleased — in view of the relaxation or repeal of the Red Brigades' solemnly declared decision to hide nothing from the people. Of course it would be naïve to think there had really been a change of attitude towards postal privacy, a true repeal. There was obviously some motive, some plan behind it all. None the less, from a given time it wasn't the Red Brigades who made Moro's letters public. And it's reasonable to assume that the zeal with which they accomplished their postal duties had no ulterior motive or scope. For it's a fact that a member of the Red Brigades risked his life in order to deliver a letter such as this:

My Dearest Noretta,
I want you to receive on Easter Day, you and all the family, my

warmest and most affectionate wishes, together with all my love
to the children and to the little one in particular. Remember me to
Anna whom I was to have seen today. I beg Agnese to keep you
company at night. I am fairly well, adequately fed and solicitously
looked after. I bless you and send my fond wishes to all. I kiss you.

Aldo

A letter which contains perhaps one item that might serve as propaganda for the Red Brigades — the fact that the prisoner was 'fairly
well, adequately fed and solicitously looked after'. And maybe he
too had his risotto, like Judge Sossi. But they didn't publish this
letter either. Moreover the Red Brigades had possibly one ethic for
before and one for after the sentence: Aldo Moro may have been seen
as a public person during the trial and thus have had no right to
privacy, but no longer such after the sentence. Once condemned to
death he was entitled to live between the verdict and its execution in a
totally personal, totally private sphere of emotions and experiences.
All the more so since the Christian Democrats were unanimously
concerned to keep Moro's emotions and experiences personal and
private by their silent and unyielding 'fin de non recevoir' of the
instructions delivered by their 'detained' President. (Indeed, each
time Moro decided to 'convene the National Council of Christian
Democrats at its earliest convenience to discuss means of freeing
their President from detention', the silence maintained by the jurists
and petty lawyers — of which there is no lack in Italy — was
amazing, considering their customary zeal in examining every point
under all its headings.) However a member of the Red Brigades
obviously took considerable risks for the simple purpose of delivering Moro's Easter greetings to his family. Though retro-
spectively and statistically we can now assert that the risk was in fact
minimal and that he could only have been intercepted by pure
accident. Indeed, considering the ineffectiveness of the Police force's
activities, the risk was practically non-existent. Yet at the time their
activities were so loudly proclaimed in the press and on radio and
television, were apparently so relentless and thorough, that it was
more than legitimate to hope — or for the Red Brigades to fear —
they would achieve some results.

Thus it is highly unlikely that Aldo Moro, when he announced
that he was well fed and well cared for, was trying to flatter his jailers
or to reassure his family. Taking into account the need for a safe

hiding-place and their restricted means, the Red Brigades did probably try to make the 'People's Prison' as different as possible from that of the SIM such as they imagined or had experienced it. A prison which didn't aim at destroying the prisoner's 'political and private identity'; a prison such as that of the Florentine Renaissance according to the *Novella del Grasso Legnaiuolo* or of Bourbon Palermo according to *I mafiosi della Vicaria*; a prison, in other words, from a time when prisons were not yet the object of theories, not yet a problem. Moreover in Moro's case it was to their advantage that his personality be freely revealed and analysed rather than suppressed and modified. Moro had to go on being himself in the 'People's Prison'. Apart from his unavoidable confinement (which involved his jailers as well), there must be no constriction, no physical, psychological or chemical intervention. And the censorship of his correspondence would have been minimal. But Moro was unaware, or suspicious of this ethic. Therefore — with the exception of one of his last published letters — his missives were desperately and lucidly self-censored, and for this purpose he tried to adapt his language of *non-communication* to his *communications*.

One of the most extraordinary stories Borges wrote is called 'Pierre Menard, Author of Don Quixote'.

Like all that which seems to be totally fantastic, pure invention and myth, this tale is based on a true fact, a reality, a precise event which, if not actually perceived by what is known as the Western World, was entirely perceptible. This event was the publication in 1905 of the *Vida de Don Quijote y Sancho* by Miguel de Unamuno. From that moment it was no longer possible to read *Don Quixote* as Cervantes had written it. Unamuno's interpretation, which seemed crystal clear as regards Cervantes' book, was in fact a reflection — of Unamuno, of Unamuno's time, of his emotions, of his vision of the world and of all that was Spanish. From then on we read Unamuno's *Don Quixote* when we think we are reading Cervantes' *Don Quixote* — indeed, reading Cervantes' *Don Quixote*.

About half a century later Borges wrote 'Pierre Menard' (and it would indeed be a truly Borgesian situation were Borges to say that he'd never thought of Unamuno). It is the story of a French writer who, apart from a slight 'visible' literary oeuvre, leaves another, unfinished but grandiose, unparalleled — and 'invisible': the creation not of a 'different' *Don Quixote* but of 'the' *Don Quixote*. Of Cervantes' *Don Quixote*. Similar in every respect. And in every respect different:

It is a revelation to compare Menard's *Don Quixote* with Cervantes'. The latter, for example, wrote (part one, chapter nine):

. . . truth, whose mother is history, rival of time, depository of deeds, witness of the past, exemplar and adviser to the present, and the future's counsellor.

Written in the seventeenth century, written by the 'lay genius' Cervantes, this enumeration is a mere rhetorical praise of history. Menard, on the other hand writes:

. . . truth, whose mother is history, rival of time, depository of deeds, witness of the past, exemplar and adviser to the present, and the future's counsellor.

History, the *mother* of truth: the idea is astounding. Menard, a contemporary of William James, does not define history as an inquiry into reality but as its origin. Historical truth, for him, is not what has happened; it is what we judge to have happened. The final phrases 'exemplar and adviser to the present, and the future's counsellor' are brazenly pragmatic.

I recalled this tale, this fable, as soon as I'd finished putting the chronicles and documents of the Moro affair into some kind of order. Here too one had the irresistible impression that the Moro affair had already been written, was already a completed literary work, already existed in all its unbearable perfection. Inviolable except in the manner of Pierre Menard — by changing everything without changing anything. And to parody Borges:

On 16 March 1978 at a few minutes to nine, Aldo Moro, President of the Christian Democratic Party, comes out of number 79, via del Forte Trionfale. The official blue 130 and his escort's small white Alfa Romeo are waiting. The President will go first to the Christian Democratic Study Centre and then, at ten o'clock, to the Chamber of Deputies where Andreotti will introduce the new Government and announce its policy. This new Government, the first Christian Democratic Government to have the support of the Communist Party, is Moro's cautious and patient creation. However there are some misgivings both within the Communist Party, dissatisfied by the presence in the new Government of former, not much respected members of the Christian Democratic Party, and within that section of Christian Democracy which is wary of the so-called 'historical compromise'.

Written, and read — immediately after Moro's abduction, this is a simple account of what Moro was doing and intended to do. On the other hand:

'On 16 March 1978 at a few minutes to nine Aldo Moro, President of the Christian Democratic Party, comes out of number 79, via del Forte Trionfale. The official blue 130 and his escort's small white Alfa Romeo are waiting. The President will go first to the

24

Christian Democratic Study Centre and then, at ten o'clock, to the Chamber of Deputies where Andreotti will introduce the new Government and announce its policy. This new Government, the first Christian Democratic Government to have the support of the Communist Party, is Moro's cautious and patient creation. However there are some misgivings both within the Communist Party, dissatisfied by the presence in the new Government of former, not much respected members of the Christian Democratic Party, and within that section of Christian Democracy which is wary of the so-called 'historical compromise'.

If today I write these words — the same and in the same order — their significance for me and for the reader will be quite different. The centre of gravity has somehow been displaced: from Moro, coming out of his home unaware of the ambush, to the Chamber of Deputies where Moro's absence will promptly achieve what his presence could only have attained with difficulty — that appeasement and harmony in which the fourth Government, presided over by Andreotti, was to be unanimously approved. The tragedy of the abduction has been replaced — and as a result of what is commonly called 'hindsight' — by the tragedy of Moro's absence (from Parliament, from politics) which will be, in a certain sense, *more positive* than his presence. As Pirandello would say: 'That, gentlemen, is the whole tragedy.'

But my intention in recalling Borges' fable was less superficial, less parodistic. Why does the Moro affair give that impression of something already written, something inhabiting a sphere of intangible literary perfection, something that can only be faithfully rewritten and, while being rewritten, be totally altered without altering anything? There are so many reasons, not all of them comprehensible. Yet it can be said that, like *Don Quixote*, the Moro affair takes place unrealistically in a real historical and contextual climate. Just as Don Quixote took his stance from the knights-errant of old, so Moro and his vicissitudes seem to have emerged from a certain literary genre. I recalled Pasolini. I might also recall two stories of mine — neither to parade nor disown them — at least two: *Il contesto* (Equal Danger) and *Todo Modo*.

In *Storia della Democrazia Cristiana* published shortly before the Moro affair, Giorgio Galli wrote:

Probably part of this governing body (Christian Democracy) —

until the 1950s typically representative of a Roman Catholic culture and background — began in the 1960s to include an increasing number of members from a different background who perhaps, though always practising Catholics, were not even really Catholics at all. None the less, the official ideology which cements the power-block Christian Democracy is increasingly becoming, is dominated by 'Eusebian' concepts and principles. When the degenerative influence resulting from this philosophy of the conservative praxis was at its peak, Leonardo Sciascia and Elio Petri synthesized, in the film *Todo Modo*, a parable of characters already epitomized in the reports of the social attitudes at this (1952) Naples conference.

A synthesis, a summing up. But in view of the superficiality, the lack of self-criticism and even of common sense against which Italian political life has evolved, such syntheses could only be forebodings and premonitions if they were not outright incitements. Indeed when the truth which had been confined to literature emerged harsh and tragic within the context of everyday life, and could no longer be ignored, it seemed as if it were a product of literature. Thus it was the men of letters (I prefer this Voltairian term to the vague, imprecise generalization 'intellectuals') who were blamed by the politicians in power, or on the periphery of power. And not without some justification, some insight, considering that at a given moment these same men of letters were to experience the hallucinatory impression that they had invented that reality.

But let us go a step further with Borges' fable. The impression that everything which occurred in the Moro affair did so, as it were, *in literature*, derives mainly from the elusiveness of the facts, a sort of withdrawal of the facts — when they occurred and even more so in retrospect — into a dimension of unfailing imaginative or fanciful consequentiality, from which a constant, stubborn ambiguity overflows. Only in fantasy, in dreams is such perfection achieved. Not in real life. Or, more prosaically: anyone can evade the Italian police in its present state of training, organization and management, but it's not so easy to evade the laws of probability. Yet according to the statements broadcast by the Minister of the Interior concerning the operations the police carried out between Moro's abduction and the discovery of his body, the Red Brigades did indeed evade the laws of probability. Which is *realistic* but can't be *really true*. (Tommaseo, *Dictionary of Synonyms*: 'For added emphasis the two are conjoined and one says: a real true fact, and such like. *Real* in this case seems to reinforce *true*, not simply as pleonasm, but thus: a real true fact hasn't simply really occurred but has occurred as it is told, as it appeared, as it is believed . . .')

Every occurrence which will later acquire significance is constituted by a complex of tiny occurrences, so small they are often imperceptible, which are drawn in a concentric irresistible motion towards an invisible centre, a vacant magnetic field where they take shape and constitute, once united, that significant occurrence. In this shape, the shape they assume together, no tiny occurrence is accidental, incidental, fortuitous — each part, however minute, has its purpose — and thus its justification — in the whole. And the whole in the parts.

In the Moro affair one of these minute facts is the expression 'a great Statesman', which is used at a given time as a substitute for the name Moro or for terms such as 'the President of the Christian Democrats', 'the Leader', 'the Great Leader', 'the brilliant Leader'. . . . The term 'Statesman' was first applied to Moro by the press on 18 March in the, probably translated, declaration of the General Secretary of the UN: 'One of Italy's most eminent statesmen.' The term recurs in the papers, but sporadically, after Moro's first communication — his letter to Cossiga, Minister of the Interior. On 18 April we find it, linked for the first time to the adjective 'great', in President Carter's communication. Though we can't tell what it sounded like in the original, it was the right word, the word that was wanted, that would make all future references to Moro involve a comparison — tacit but unavoidable — between what he had been and what he now was. He had been 'a Great Statesman'. And now he was nothing but a man 'under full and absolute control' (according to his own words in the first letter from the 'People's Prison' — words which were to be the most widely quoted until well after the end of the affair).

A 'Statesman' is specifically a man of the State — a man who dedicates to the State, to that structure which is the State and to the laws that govern it, his considered allegiance, his thoughts and his care. And a 'Great Statesman' is obviously a man who dedicates such qualities and activities superlatively. And how could this image of the 'Great Statesman' be identified with the Moro who sent out messages from the 'People's Prison'? The Red Brigades had annihilated it. Instead of the 'Great Statesman' here was a man — probably subjected to physical torture, drugged and, indisputably, under the constant, obsessive threat of being put to death — who had lost that 'sense of the State' which, during more than thirty years of political activity, had so outstandingly characterized him.

This was just another blatant lie, among the many that proliferated at that time. Neither Moro nor the Party he presided over had ever had a 'sense of the State'. The idea of the State, as it had first been threateningly bandied about by some representatives of the Italian Communist Party during the previous Spring — an idea which seemed to derive, and perhaps, for reasons we shall not go into here, did derive from a position rather to the right than to the left of Hegel — had probably only crossed Aldo Moro's mind in his early youth when he took part in the cultural competitions the Fascist regime organized (the *Littorali*, where the winners were proclaimed *Littori*) and had left no trace in his thoughts — or in his concept, if we care to admit that he had a clear and definite concept, of political theory and political practice. And it isn't hard to imagine the significance of such an idea for his followers and disciples, assuredly less well equipped with concepts — or even with minds. For indeed what attracts at least one third of the Italian electorate to the Christian Democratic Party is precisely its total, reassuring — not to say invigorating — lack of an idea of the State.

In fact the attack launched the previous year by certain representatives of the Italian Communist Party against anyone who didn't manifest a passionate attachment to the State, the Italian State such as it was, served as prelude to that melodrama of devotion to the State so spectacularly enacted on the Italian stage between 16 March and 9 May 1978. And the victims of this spectacular production — crushed, as it were, by the monumental wings, the monumental backdrop — appeared to have been those who felt no particular devotion to the State, the Italian State such as it was. But the true victim was Aldo Moro.

Before 16 March Aldo Moro hadn't been a 'Great Statesman'. He had been, and continued to be even in the 'People's Prison', a great politician, careful, shrewd, calculating, seemingly pliant but in fact unyielding; patient, but with a patience bordering on stubbornness;

and he had the profoundest, most assured understanding of the natural vices and virtues of the Italian people any politician has ever had. It was precisely in this that he was unique — in his understanding of these vices and his policy of pandering to them, while enabling those who had such vices to believe they had become virtues. Such a policy combines two traditions — atavistic and individual: Italian Roman Catholicism and that crudest and most violent aspect of Italian Roman Catholicism which is social (or asocial) existence in the South of Italy. A policy similar in its consequences to the one Kutuzov adopted with Napoleon. And Moro in his prime reminded me not infrequently of Kutuzov as Tolstoy represented him in *War and Peace*. For instance, chapter XV, Part One, where Prince Andrew sees Kutuzov once again, his air of facial and bodily weariness unchanged; or Kutuzov listening with an air of weary irony to Denisov expounding his plan to save the country by cutting off Napoleon's supply route, and then interrupting him to ask if he is related to General Superintendent Denisov; or Kutuzov who 'knew something more which would decide the issue of the war' — something more which was not related to relatively rational plans but to the geography and behaviour of the Russian people.

Moro, seen on television, seemed overcome by an immensely ancient weariness, an unfathomable boredom. Only occasionally, at the corners of his mouth, in his eyes, was a glint of irony or scorn perceptible — promptly to be extinguished by weariness, by boredom. Yet one felt that 'he knew something more' — the Italian and Roman Catholic art of squandering the new on the old, of making every innovation serve old purposes and, especially, of seeing human nature negatively, negativistically. Which was for him both an affliction and a weapon. A weapon he was obviously reluctant to exploit, but exploited. He was, as Pasolini said, 'the least implicated of all'. But precisely the fact that he was the least implicated gave him the indisputable and even welcome authority over the members of the Christian Democratic Party to speak for them all — an asset but also a sacrifice. And outside Christian Democracy, in the eyes of the other parties and of all Italy, this peculiarity made him, almost pathetically, more credible, more trustworthy.

If Moro ever had an idea which resembled the idea of the State, such an idea was, as it were, bricked up within Christian Democracy, within the medieval citadel of Christian Democracy which seemed to be open and defenceless but which, at the onset of danger, turned out to be adequately provided for, well guarded and fortified. Some evidence of such an idea can be found in his last Parliamentary address in defence of Senator Gui, who as Minister of Defence was accused of having participated in and benefited from a serious malpractice. It is worth quoting a few telling passages:

In this attitude [of defending Senator Gui] Christian Democracy stands united and by it we signify our defence of Christian Democracy as a whole. We have sometimes been divided, but in small matters, controversial matters. Whenever it was a question of major problems, major decisions, major principles we have never been divided — though perhaps others have split away, proving the fact that the area of truth is, objectively, vaster than our personal convictions. Thus, united we defend Christian Democracy . . . It is not a matter of a Christian Democratic superiority of any sort — a superiority which facts clearly demonstrate, significant facts because they are permanent and thus prove that they have historical and not incidental roots . . . What we refuse to accept is that our total experiment should be branded with a stigma of infamy in this nasty sequel to a bitter electoral campaign. We stand truly united in our rejection of the charge that in us everyone and everything is blameworthy. I don't know how many are involved in this political scheme but, quite frankly, it belies any attitude of democratic collaboration. [This is a warning addressed to the Communists — somewhat super-fluously since, although they wanted Gui to be taken to court, they were far from seeking to prosecute the Christian Democratic Party.] To whoever seeks to overthrow our experiment as a whole; to whoever seeks to attack our ethic and our policy in public, as has been cynically suggested, we reply with firm resolution and by an appeal to public opinion which found us not guilty of historical crimes and did not want our power to wane . . . If you have any sense at all — which at times one is tempted to doubt — we strongly advise you not to underestimate the great authority of public opinion which, for over three decades, has found in Christian Democracy its expression and its justification. I believe that it has no intention of renouncing this mode of rep-resentation, just as we would never consider renouncing the authority, the privileges it entails or the responsibilities with which we are entrusted. These are extremely serious matters and it is our duty at this juncture to reassert the Nation's right to freedom and integrity in its social and political essence.

Or to express the gist of President Moro's speech: the Nation's freedom and integrity are sacred; Christian Democracy represents the Nation's freedom and integrity; Christian Democracy is sacred. A syllogism from which another can be derived: the unwavering electoral consensus is proof that Christian Democracy is innocent; Senator Gui is a Christian Democrat; Senator Gui is innocent. And Senator Gui may well be innocent of the specific charges brought against him. But these syllogisms can't possibly prove his innocence. These syllogisms which transcend the question of Senator Gui's guilt or innocence only assert once and for all Christian Democracy's innocence and that, whenever required, this innocence can serve as guarantee for the innocence of each member.

Beyle believed that a Republic of good Christians could not survive. Montesquieu amended: 'A Republic of good Christians cannot exist.' But a Republic of good Italian Roman Catholics can exist and survive. Thus.

To this Christian Democracy that recovers its unity and solidarity in defending an individual Christian Democrat; to this family party; to this party which interprets and represents the nation's 'common goal' even though it represents numerically one third of the population, Aldo Moro addresses himself from the 'People's Prison'.

His first letter arrives on the evening of 29 March, delivered by the Red Brigades together with their third communiqué. It is addressed to the Minister of the Interior, Francesco Cossiga. Moro writes 'with great caution'. Obviously such caution has been dictated to him by his jailers. But the Red Brigades explain: 'He asked to write a private letter (secret manoeuvres are the norm with the Christian Democratic Mafia) to the Government and more particularly to the Chief Copper Cassiga. His request was granted but, since nothing should be hidden from the people according to our custom, we are making it public.' His request to write a letter was granted, but not to write a private letter — even though its privacy had been guaranteed. And that makes a difference.

The first problem to be solved is why he wrote to the Minister of the Interior. The most natural recipient for Moro's proposal would have been the Minister of Justice. Or, if he did indeed possess that 'sense of the State' with which the press was already beginning to endow him, he should have turned to the Head of the Cabinet or to the President of the Republic. Why then to the Minister of the Interior? That of all his 'friends' he considered him to be the most faithful isn't a sufficient answer. There isn't a passage in the letter which is addressed to Cossiga personally whether as Christian Democrat or as friend. One might presume, however, that there are certain passages addressed to Cossiga as Minister of the Interior, as Chief Copper, to quote the Red Brigades.

Dear Francesco,
Together with my warmest greetings I am constrained by painful

circumstances to inform you, while taking into account your responsibilities (for which I have the utmost regard) of certain clear and realistic facts. I purposely refrain from mentioning my feelings and shall stick to facts. Although I know nothing either of what occurred after my abduction or of how it came about, it is certain — I have been explicitly informed of this — that I am seen as a political prisoner subject, as President of the Christian Democratic Party, to a trial aimed at exposing my responsibilities over the past thirty years (a trial at present restricted to political terms, which grows more threatening every day).

Under these circumstances I am writing to you with great restraint, so that you and our comrades with the Cabinet President at their head (and obviously keeping the President of the Republic informed) may consider at your convenience what should be done to avoid worse disasters.

Therefore examine the case thoroughly before the situation gets out of hand. As I see it, the serious charge which is being brought against me concerns me in my capacity as official representative of the Christian Democratic Party as a whole in the administration of its political programme. In fact we members of the Party in office are all implicated and it is our collective conduct which is on trial and for which I must answer. In the above circumstances — apart from any humanitarian considerations, which however cannot be overlooked — what is at stake is the *raison d'Etat*. And in view of my aforementioned present predicament, this *raison d'Etat* signifies primarily that I am under the full and absolute control of my captors, subjected to a verdict of the people which could be opportunely modified, that I find myself in such circumstances in possession of a vast knowledge and understanding derived from my long experience and in danger of being asked or induced to speak in a way that might be detrimental and dangerous in certain eventualities.

Moreover, the principle according to which the demands of kidnappers should not be met — a principle which is questionable even in ordinary circumstances when the victim's life may be at stake — is not valid in political cases where inevitable and incalculable damage would ensue not to the victim alone but to the State. The sacrifice of innocent lives in the name of an abstract legal principle is inadmissible when an obvious state of emergency should make their deliverance unquestionable. There

34

is not a State — apart from Israel and Germany (except in the case of Lorenz) — which has not acted positively. And let it not be said that the State loses face because it is not able to prevent the kidnapping of an eminent personality who has a part to play in the existence of the State.

To recall briefly the attitude of States in the past, I would remind you of the exchanges of prisoners between Brezhnev and Pinochet, the countless exchanges of spies, the extradition of dissidents from Soviet territory. I am well aware that such an action is painful but the fatal consequences of avoiding it must be envisaged. In guerilla warfare such are the alternatives which arise and have to be objectively and unemotionally assessed, while considering the political issue at stake. Might not a preventive intervention from the Vatican (or from elsewhere? Where?) be opportune? It is essential that, with the President of the Cabinet's consent, contact should be maintained with a restricted number of qualified political personalities to persuade those who might be reluctant. A hostile attitude would be unproductive and misguided.

May God inspire you to act for the best and to avoid becoming involved in a painful incident which might have unforeseen consequences. My most affectionate greetings.

For Poe's protagonist Charles Auguste Dupin, it was essential, when investigating a crime, to be able to identify with the criminal. A very sound precept not only in detective novels but also in real life. But one which, none the less, is totally rejected by every self-respecting police force. In the Moro affair a double identification was required: with the Red Brigades (whose complete immunity and security when performing the riskiest actions, more often than not simply to deride or impress their adversaries, is not unrelated to what Dupin, in 'The Purloined Letter', calls the *invisibility of the obvious*) and with Moro, the captive who sent messages from his captivity to be deciphered on the basis of what his 'friends' knew about him — his thoughts, behaviour, habits and idiosyncrasies — and by accurately imagining what it was like to be in the circumstances in which he found himself.

The first stage of such an identification could only be an attempt to understand what might be the feelings of a man who, after about two weeks of solitude, exhausted by interrogations and sleeplessness yet

35

still perfectly lucid — probably with that lucidity caused by extreme exhaustion — finally has a chance to write to someone who had both the power and the means to free him from these conditions. Albeit a cautious, reticent, enigmatic letter that says what the jailers want him to say while hinting at those things which they would not allow him to mention. And most likely he had thought it over for hours on end during his sleepless nights, awaiting the moment when he would be allowed to write. As many hours as his 'friends' and the police should have spent deciphering it. And most likely too the censorship, if it existed, would have been minimal in view of the Red Brigades' belief that Moro had understood what they were up to, and that in exchange for this tiny and precarious margin of liberty he would play their game. Whether he had always held the opinion that it was right and necessary for a State to negotiate an exchange of prisoners with terrorists, or had only come to accept it to save his own life, or again was pretending to have accepted it, one thing is certain: had Moro not shown that he was willing to assist the Red Brigades' blackmail, no letter from him would ever have been forwarded from the 'People's Prison'. And it seems obvious to me that, at least when he wrote to Cossiga, and precisely because his letter was addressed to the Minister of the Interior, Moro was still relying on some decisive (and intelligent) action by the police — that his plea for negotiations and exchange was, for this great pro-crastinator, the one and only way of gaining time — while he trusted, or at least hoped, that the police would not waste theirs. But the police did waste it. More lavishly than Moro could ever have imagined.

Assuming therefore that Moro was addressing himself to Cossiga in his capacity as Minister of the Interior (and not because, of all his 'friends' he was the most faithful or because he was, as it were, the chief decision maker) it follows that he must have tried to convey in this letter any clues he had chanced upon which might help to direct the search to his whereabouts.

If we exclude the possibility that the letter contained cryptograms or might be deciphered by means of a spy code to be de-constructed and re-constructed, then a simple, ordinary code might be used — what could be described as the code of meaninglessness or nonsense; and the most nonsensical passage in the letter is this: 'Might not a preventive intervention from the Vatican (or from elsewhere? Where?) be opportune?' An intervention from the Vatican to the Red

Brigades? What could be more absurd? And what does 'preventive' mean?

Let's try to put ourselves in Moro's place. In view of the position he occupies and the moment at which he was kidnapped — a moment when the majority was about to ratify in Parliament his most crafty and patient political stratagem — Moro is convinced that the police have been mobilized as never before and launched on a vast and intricate action, a spectacularly massive and meticulous campaign. Furthermore, in view of the time it took to travel from the site of the kidnapping to the 'People's Prison' (it seems improbable that the Red Brigades, foreseeing the repercussions, would have made a detour for the sole purpose of disorientating their captive), he knows he is still in Rome — and probably this knowledge is confirmed by noises his jailers can't prevent him from overhearing — traffic, church bells, voices filtering through . . . Putting together what he knows and what he assumes, he can but ask himself this question: How is it possible that the police are unable to locate the 'People's Prison'? The answer to which would be that the 'People's Prison' is located in some unsuspected place, a place beyond suspicion, a place to which the police does not have access, a place whose immunity is respected. Vatican City? Some embassy?

We don't want to suggest that Moro was, in fact, in Vatican City or some embassy. Only that he may have believed he was — because of his illusions concerning the efficiency of the police and the intelligence and good will of his 'friends'. For my part I'm convinced that the 'People's Prison' also partook of what we called the *invisibility of the obvious* and others have called *over-obviousness*. The 'People's Prison' owed its immunity partly if not entirely to the obviousness of its location. But an obviousness linked to other obviousnesses, all of them conforming to the Red Brigades' concept of the clandestine.

However romantic it might seem to suppose that Moro's first letter contained some clue which could have helped the police, let us not forget that it was addressed to the Minister of the Interior; that the reference to the Vatican, incongruous as it is, is the only reference to a place which could be a hiding-place; that it is the only passage where his rational tone becomes somewhat urgent, somewhat dramatic (it would be too easy — and too difficult — to explain away those two desperate question-marks literally as a hesitant quest for mediators). Furthermore Moro knows perfectly well that, if necessary, he would be the best possible mediator; just as he knows that an organization such as Amnesty International would be better able to negotiate with the Red Brigades than the Holy See.

And there is one thing more to be said about this letter to Cossiga: had Moro written no other, it might today be read as an urge to be firm, not to yield to blackmail, not to negotiate. A number of details, considered independently, could be interpreted in this way; not least the somewhat unexpected reference to the exchange of prisoners between Brezhnev and Pinochet — that is, between two regimes he didn't fancy. But perhaps what Moro meant to imply was that negotiations and concessions should be considered as a last resort — the essential thing was to gain time, let things drag on — until he was found.

On the day Moro is kidnapped, the leader of the Republican Party, Ugo de Malfa, declares: 'This is a challenge to the Democratic State. The State accepts the challenge.' National rhetoric — spent embers under the ashes — flares up once again. The headline 'The Nation accepts the challenge' epitomises it — but acquires tragi-comic overtones when read four months later with no more to boast of than the arrest of a single Red Brigades' member — a certain Cristoforo Piancone, wounded by a jailer, Lorenzo Cotungo, before the latter collapsed and died.

Nor was Mrs Eleonora Moro to escape the flood of rhetoric. The words: 'My husband is not to be bartered whatever happens' are put into her mouth; she becomes the Classical Roman heroine and proof that 'in the Italian heart Roman courage still survives'. Mrs Moro denies, declining such an honour. But must we impute the invention to a simple flare of rhetoric? Isn't it precisely from then, from that moment, from that falsehood, that intransigence and relentlessness come into play? But whether motivated by rhetoric or cold-blooded expediency, any attempt to turn her into a Volumnia — as confronting the Coriolanus Moro, begging to be bartered, she would become — is promptly rejected by Mrs Eleanora Moro. However, such beautiful and especially such useful words should not be wasted. And, since her uncompromising denial makes it impossible to assign them to her any longer, it is rumoured that she is unquestionably capable of these unspoken words, that they are not beyond her and that they are in fact 'implied in the highly moral dignity of her behaviour'. And this was only one of the ghastly hoaxes mounted around the 'affair' to make it the more ghastly — so that one experiences a kind of reflected shame at simply continuing to peruse the documents.

All the mechanisms that have to be set in motion against the 'abominable blackmail' are serviced and oiled in preparation for the 'abominable blackmail' to materialize. But there is no mention of it in the Red Brigades' first communiqué delivered to one of the Roman newspapers on 18 March, together with a photograph of Moro (Moro with the Red Brigades' banner as backdrop and the expression of weary boredom, the flicker of irony so familiar to thousands of viewers). Nor is it mentioned in the second. Nor in the third which accompanies Moro's letter to Cossiga. The Red Brigades have contrived to make it look as if the 'abominable black-mail' were Moro's idea and requested by him alone. Probably by telling him that they had already communicated their conditions — but to no avail; that it was now up to him to persuade his 'friends'.

The Red Brigades' deceit, the trick they'd played on Moro, can easily be assumed from the tone of Moro's letter to Cossiga: the tone of someone carrying on a discussion begun by others or breaking into it. Yet as far as I can see, no one has taken the trouble to point this out. It was in the Red Brigades' interest that Moro should appear as the originator and main supporter of the request for an exchange of prisoners (to which they would eventually comply, out of clemency, by commuting the death sentence); that he should live in the mean time in terror of the trial. The Government, on the other hand, had every reason to make the most of the psychological and moral havoc the Red Brigades had wrought on Moro, reducing the proud owner of a 'sense of the State', the 'Great Statesman' to beg the State to renounce its own essence and role!

But what did Moro really think and want?

In the first place he wanted the police to find him. Thus negotiations — long and protracted negotiations — would, as ever, have seemed to him the only way to compensate for their in-adequacies and blunders and enable them finally to locate the 'People's Prison' — whether owing to the sheer dimensions of the operation or to information gleaned or to pure chance. In the mean-time, for as long as his 'friends' kept the negotiations going and the police went about their job, he intended to refute the accusations, resist the trial — as the men of the Red Brigades were doing in Turin.

For, despite the Red Brigades' statement in their third com-muniqué, it seems obvious that Moro didn't accept the accusations, that 'the prisoner's total collaboration' was a mere rhetorical figure. This emerges not only from the sixth communiqué dated 19 April but also from what Moro says to Cossiga, which can reasonably be read to imply that, although for the moment the trial is political and thus no more than an examination of his policy, which he can cope with, it will grow more pressing when it comes to specific facts involving specific and personal responsibilities. Then, despite his intention not to collaborate, the fact that he is 'under their full and absolute control' and that they have the means to induce him to 'speak in a way that might be detrimental and dangerous', should not be forgotten. This isn't blackmail but foresight and prudence.

Furthermore, quite apart from any delays and procrastinations to help the police, Moro believed that an exchange of prisoners was 'realistically' acceptable — on the basis, that is, of reality's power to make what is theoretically unacceptable and impossible practically acceptable and possible. And even if this wasn't always the case, it was so at least when a man's life was at stake. When a man's life is weighed against abstract principles, can a Christian hesitate?

He had already expressed such an opinion among his 'friends' when discussing political kidnappings as against kidnappings where money is the motive. Why shouldn't he confirm it and defend it in his own case?

The Moro who says:

. . . the principle according to which kidnapping must not bear fruit — questionable even in normal cases when the victim is most likely to suffer from it — is not valid in political cases when inevitable and incalculable damage will ensue not to the victim alone but to the State;

the Moro who says this is perfectly consistent with the politician and teacher the Italian people have known for some thirty years. Consistent with his view of life, of Italy, of politics; with his sense of justice and his sense of the State (not this time between inverted commas — a different sense of the State from that which had been treacherously foisted upon him).

I don't think he was afraid of death. Of *that* death, perhaps — but it was still life he was afraid of. 'Centuries of sirocco' someone said, 'are in his gaze.' But also centuries of death. Of contemplating death, of familiarity with death. Ronchey wrote: 'He's the embodiment of Southern pessimism.' What is Southern pessimism? In what does it consist? In seeing each thing, each thought, each illusion — even the thoughts and illusions which seem to make the world go round — flow towards death. Everything flows towards death — except the thought of death, the idea of death. 'Nothing but one thought, the thought of death is true thought.' It infiltrates all things, like the sirocco — in the land of the sirocco.

I think it was around the seventeenth century that Sicilian noblemen had a cunning contrivance built into their houses, a sirocco room, a room in which to take refuge when the sirocco blew. Or was it a room in which to take refuge, in which to shelter from the thought of death? But I don't suppose such rooms were really much use against the sirocco — before it can be felt in the air the sirocco has already taken possession of our minds, our knees.

I don't think he was afraid of death. But of *that* death . . . 'Who said human nature is capable of bearing it without going mad? What is the point of such a monstrous, meaningless, vain outrage? Perhaps a man exists to whom the verdict was read out, who was allowed ample time for self-torture and to whom it was then said: Go. You have been reprieved! Well, that man could perhaps tell us. Christ too spoke of this anguish, this horror. No. It's not fair to treat a man like that.'

He was treated like that. Worse than that — in a murky, dark, underhand parody of a *legal murder*. There was no reason sufficient in itself for not doing all that was possible to stop it from happening — especially not what is called the *raison d'Etat*, of a State which had abolished the anguish and horror of the death penalty.

Moro endured it without going mad. He wasn't a hero nor was he trained for heroism. He didn't want to die *that* death and he tried to avoid it. But there was besides, in his not wanting to die, not *that* death, a concern, an obsession with something more than his own life (and his own death). And this concern, this obsession may perhaps justify the title 'Great Statesman' which, in the world outside at that time, for the wrong reasons and in the wrong sense, was being foisted upon him. And he was so far from being a 'Statesman' in that other sense that his references to the State and to reasons of State in the letter to Cossiga and in others that followed imply something totally opposed to an entity oblivious of and above persons, individuals, with their peculiarities and their identities. The State with which he is concerned, the State that occupies his thoughts obsessively, is, I believe, what he implies when he uses the word family. That it isn't a mere substitution — the word family for the word State — but more an extension of its meaning: from his own family to the family of the Party and to the family of the Nation of which the Party represents, even for those who haven't voted for it, the 'general consensus'. And in this 'general consensus' there is, according to Moro's concept, just one thing which is sure and certain and must be maintained at all cost, within the fluidity of concessions and conflicts, and that thing is liberty.

Moro, in the 'People's Prison' saw liberty threatened and realized from whence such a threat came, by whom and how it is brought about. He may even have identified himself as a 'carrier' — like the carriers of certain diseases who carry the infection without themselves being sick. Whence his impatience to get out of the 'People's Prison' so as to impart what he had discovered, what he now knew. 'Had I not a family so dependent on me it might be somewhat different,' he says in his second letter addressed to Zaccagnini. 'Somewhat different' mind. Not all that different, to die or to go on living. But his family needs him, needs him badly. And he will repeat it in each of his letters until the letter to the President of the Republic when their dependence becomes 'serious and urgent'.

Now this constant reference to his family's dependence on him, a serious and urgent dependence was, Moro surely realized, overtly denied by his family's material circumstances — its dependence on him, on his return was purely psychological, not material or social. Moreover as a Southerner he could hardly have considered a family like his own to be dependent — it depended on him neither for funds nor protection. A Southerner whose sons have good jobs and whose daughters, apart from their jobs, have good husbands; who leaves his wife with a roof over her head and a pension and the whole family with a respectable name would see himself as free from family responsibilities and quits with life and with death. All of which suggests that if Moro continued to harp on the family's dependence it is precisely because it was so obviously and materially refuted. Because he wanted it to be understood that he was referring to something quite different. And when he says 'It is a known fact that my family's most urgent problems are the main reason for my struggle against death' (in the letter delivered to *Il Messaggero* on 29 April), he is trying to convey that by thus referring to a fact that isn't 'known', there must be some other reason for his struggle against death. Furthermore in his letters to his family — at least in those which have been published — there is nothing to indicate actual family problems. It might be objected that he mentions the family with that emotiveness, that sentimentality and reverence which is considered to be typically Italian and confirms the saying: 'On an Italian's flag are the words *I have a family*'; but that would be to underestimate Moro's intelligence, his restraint, his lucidity, qualities which emerge from his letters written in the 'People's Prison' more than from anything he did during his three decades of political activity.

A letter from Moro to Zaccagnini reaches the editorial office of *La Republica* on the afternoon of 4 April, together with the Red Brigades' fourth communiqué and a printed pamphlet which includes their *Risoluzione della direzione strategica*.

If the Red Brigades are resorting to wider means of publicity for their projected policy — which according to the rules of strategy ought to be communicated only to their members — it is probably because, apart from the obvious advantages of over-exposure, they want to reach, precisely by using the publicity service of the S.I.M. (Military Information Service), sympathisers who are still wavering but more or less united. For the *Risoluzione* has a chance of being received with enthusiasm only by such sympathisers as are dispersed here and there. And it might indeed be read to some advantage by the police — but that is highly unlikely.

Moro's letter provokes an immediate and not unexpected response — the joint effort of a select group of Christian Democrat notables, officially communicated to the Party organ and reprinted the following day by all the papers:

> As our readers will see, the contents of this letter signed by Aldo Moro and addressed to Senator Zaccagnini, reveal once again the conditions of total coercion in which such documents are written and confirm our fear that this letter too cannot be ascribed to him ethically.

Those readers — at any rate the few or many who understand what they read — didn't agree with the Christian Democrat notables, even if the press and television did. Whether they approved or not of Moro's attitude, the public couldn't see why a man should be considered 'out of his mind' and in no condition to comprehend and decide for himself simply because he doesn't want to die and asks his own political party to ransom him by means which, even if they might not serve electoral propaganda, are not in the realm of the impossible. There were of course the five victims — the five members of Moro's escort killed at the time of his kidnapping, but, after all, did five corpses warrant a sixth?

Moreover Moro's letter didn't seem unreasonable. Nor was it.

Dear Zaccagnini,

I write to you wishing to include Piccoli, Bartolomei, Galloni, Gaspari, Fanfani, Andreotti and Cossiga to whom you will please read this letter and with whom you will assume responsibilities which are both personal and collective. I address myself above all to the Christian Democratic Party, accused in the name of all its members — accusations for which I am required to bear consequences that are not hard to imagine. Of course other Parties are also involved. But a moral problem of this magnitude concerns above all the Christian Democrats who must act, whatever the others say, whatever their immediate objections. I refer primarily to the Communist Party which, even were it to advocate firmness, cannot forget that my tragic abduction occurred as we were on our way to the Cabinet to consecrate the Government I had taken such pains to constitute. Moreover, it is only right that, in summing up this painful business, I should recall my extreme, repeated and justified reluctance to assume the charge of President which you offered me and which now snatches me from my family at a time when it has the utmost need of me. Morally it is you who are in the situation that I occupy in fact. And finally, at this critical juncture I am obliged to add that if my escort had not been, for administrative reasons, in every way inadequate to the circumstances, I might not now be here.

All that is over and done with. As for the present, I am subjected to an arduous political trial which will have foreseeable repercussions and consequences.

I am a political prisoner whom your sudden decision to break off all negotiations involving others who are likewise in custody, has put in an intolerable position. Time is running out and there is, alas, barely enough left. At any moment it may be too late. What we are discussing here is not legal theory (although laws concerning cases of necessity exist), but whether, from a humane and political point of view, it would not be possible to see my problem realistically, giving it the only positive solution possible, which is to consider the liberation of prisoners on both sides and concentrate on the purely political context of the matter. To hold out may seem more proper, but certain concessions would be not only just but even politically rewarding.

As I have said, a great many States conform to such a civilized attitude. If no one else has the courage to do so, let the Christian Democrats, renowned for their ability to find the right solution in the most critical situations, do it. If this is not to be, you yourselves will have wished it and I can say, without rancour, that Party and individuals alike will be held responsible for the inevitable consequences. Another cycle will ensue, more terrible and no less intractable. I wish to make it clear that I say all this in perfect lucidity of mind and without having undergone personal coercion; as much lucidity, that is, as a man can have who has spent fifteen days under exceptional circumstances, who has no one to reassure him and who knows what awaits him. And to tell the truth, I feel you have let me down somewhat. Moreover my opinion has already been communicated to Taviani concerning the Sossi affair and to Gui with regards to the challenging of a law against abductions. Now that I have informed and advised you as I thought fit I shall commune with God, with those who are dear to me and with myself. Had I not a family so dependent on me things might be slightly different. But in the present circumstances it requires real courage to pay for the whole Christian Democratic Party to which I have dedicated myself without stint. May God enlighten you and do so quickly, for speed is of the essence. My warmest greetings.

According to the theory he always championed — the non-intervention of other political powers into that 'island' which is Christian Democracy — it is still on the Party he relies and, individually, on each of the seven members who, together with Zaccagnini can 'assume responsibilities', take decisions. Cossiga figures rather incongruously among the eight — Andreotti, the President of the Cabinet could have represented the Government alone; and as regards negotiations and exchanges, the Minister of Justice's inclusion would have been more expedient. Why does Moro want to include Cossiga in this select committee? Obviously so that the Minister of the Interior may decide either that the investigations and search have come to a dead end and that it is thus necessary to resort to negotiations without further delay; or that the police are on the point of success and that it is therefore opportune to hold out and not negotiate — or only negotiate to gain time.

At this point, after about twenty days in captivity, Moro can't have much hope of being found and saved by the police. He relies more on negotiations, on exchanges; and he provides the Party with an argument to justify their action before the other Parties and public opinion — should Christian Democracy require justification — that he has always approved this procedure which is consistent with his Christian faith. Some years before, Aldo Moro, President of the Christian Democratic Party, was already of the opinion that when it is a question of saving a man's life or being faithful to abstract principles, the legal concept of a *state of necessity* should be enforced as a precept — the non-abstract principle of saving a human life against every abstract principle. And Christian Democrats, insofar as they were or professed to be Christians, could not think otherwise — from the first to the last.

But an unsuspected and ruthless State-idolatry seems to have suddenly possessed Christian Democracy. Moro, still holding the opinions he had always held, has become a foreign body, a kind of painful gall-stone which has to be excised — with State-idolatry as anaesthetic — from an organism which has acquired, as though by miracle, the attitudes and habits of a 'sense of the State'. Of course the fact that Moro had *always had these views* is most inconvenient — that it isn't the Red Brigades who, through torture and drugs, have made him welcome the possibility of prisoner swapping between a lawful State and a band of hooligans. But there's a remedy — and it's not hard to administer. Independent and Party dailies, the radio and television, are more or less unanimous in backing the State and proclaiming Moro's metamorphosis, his moral extinction.

It's as if a dying man had risen from his bed, leapt into the air to swing from the chandelier like Tarzan from the liana, then rushed to the window and vaulted out to land, hale and hearty, in the street. The Italian State has revived. The Italian State is alive and strong, safe and sound. For a century, for over a century it has consorted with the Sicilian Mafia, the Neapolitan Camorra, the Sardinian bandits. For three decades it has exploited corruption and incompetence, wasted public funds in streams and rivulets of unpunished embezzlement and fraud. For ten years it has quietly accepted what de Gaulle, while putting an end to it, called 'recreation' — schools occupied and vandalized and acts of juvenile violence against comrades and teachers alike. But now, confronted with Moro's sequestration by the Red Brigades, the Italian State rises up strong and impressive. Who dares question its strength, its impressiveness? No one. And least of all Moro in the 'People's Prison'.

Nenni had said: 'The Italian State is strong with the weak and weak with the strong'. Who are the weak today? Moro, his wife and children, those who think the State should have been and must be strong with the strong.

'The State's unexpected stance as 'a solid tower that will not collapse' takes Moro by surprise. How did this iron-clad, fully armoured monster emerge from that larva? Is it the 'others' who have fired Christian Democracy with such immovable steadfastness in the defence of the State? The 'others': 'I refer primarily to the Communist Party which, even were it to advocate firmness, cannot forget that my tragic abduction occurred as we were on our way to the Cabinet to consecrate the Government I had taken such pains to constitute.' But that's precisely what the Communist Party didn't forget; as Moro was soon to perceive. Meanwhile Moro, vindicating the value of such a constitution, unconsciously uses the term 'to consecrate'. A lapsus on the part of the Catholic or a premonition for the man who feels he has been 'slightly let down' (not to say totally let down)? The Catholic compiler of the Tommaseo Dictionary says: 'This lofty term should not be used for merely human matters . . . *to consecrate* is to make sacred by formal words, deeds and rites what was not sacred.' Formal words: the defence of the State. Rites: the murder of five men, the execution of a death sentence.

Two Stalinisms are in conflict — and I use the handy, contemporary word for something far older, 'something' which has always served a few inhuman human beings to indoctrinate the minds and emotions of men and wring suffering and blood from them. Or rather, it is the two halves of one and the same thing which are in conflict. And they are slowly, inexorably joining up again to squash anyone who happens to stand between them. The conscious, overt, violent and ruthless Stalinism of the Red Brigades who execute without trial those who serve the State and, after a trial, the leaders of the State. And the insidious, crafty Stalinism which treats individuals and events as if they were palimpsests, erasing what was written and rewriting it to serve their cause.

Moro doesn't want to be squashed. Not because he's a coward but, as it were, from a sense of duty. There's a kind of bureaucratic impassivity, of formality in the conclusion of his letter to Zaccagnini: 'Now that I have informed and advised you . . .' But where is that information tucked away? Probably in all that the letter doesn't and should contain — an expression of pity, of regret for the escort he saw murdered. 'And finally at this critical juncture I am obliged to add that if my escort had not been, for administrative reasons, in every way inadequate to the circumstances, I might not now be here.' An obligation — not a protest, not a complaint. And at this 'critical juncture', at the moment of truth. The words 'critical juncture' followed by the reference to the self-evident fact that the escort was inadequate seem quite *inappropriate*. Furthermore the escort's inadequacy cost them their lives. And if Moro wanted to suggest with the words 'for administrative reasons' that there were omissions and culpabilities to be sought on a higher level than that of the five men, all the more reason for him to express some pity for them.

He was not a cynic. Had he been, he would have exploited the favourable impression a word of compassion for the five murdered men would have made on public opinion. Instead he purposely denies himself this advantage. Why? Police Constable Domenico Ricci had been his chauffeur for around twenty years; Police

Inspector Oreste Leonardi had been with him for fifteen. It seems incredible that some kind of relationship shouldn't have been established between them. Yet he hasn't a word of regret for these men killed under his eyes. Why? Perhaps precisely to make his 'friends' — and Cossiga in particular — ask this question and try to answer it.

One could say that he was only vaguely aware of the lightning sequence of events that occurred in via Fani. But however rapid the action, he surely had time to realize that Leonardi and Ricci, both in his own car, had been shot dead. Furthermore he read the papers. For he was given them to read, not only because of the prison ethic mentioned earlier, but also because there was nothing in the papers to comfort him, to encourage him to resist, to make him feel that he had to defend something worth defending.

But this passage of the letter must remain shrouded in mystery — and silence. At least until someone from among the *dramatis personae* on one side or the other will be unable to resist any longer the urge to confess or the pleasure of recounting.

Of the two 'friends' Moro, in his letter to Zaccagnini, invokes as witnesses, Gui confirms the fact that Moro has always upheld the citizen's duty to pay ransom and the State's to accept an exchange of prisoners. But Taviani denies it.

And, apart from Gui's confirmation, the fact that Moro would hardly appeal to a 'friend' he knows isn't all that much a friend to confirm something that isn't true, makes Taviani's denial futile and pitiable. He may be credited with amnesia but not with veracity. Veracity is Moro's. And indeed his reaction is that of a man who, finding himself unhappy and impotent, is felled by a lie when he relied on the truth to save him.

The news has penetrated even to where I am that Taviani denies the purely incidental remark I made in my second letter, that my ideas concerning the exchange of prisoners (in circumstances such as the present) and ways of dealing with kidnappings were already known both to Taviani and to Gui. This Senator Gui correctly confirms. Senator Taviani, on the other hand, denies it without, apparently, feeling any scruple at challenging the word of an absent colleague who finds himself in difficulties and enjoys few and irregular means of communicating with the outside world. Why this contradiction? There can be only one reason: his over-eagerness — that is, his fear of not being in the forefront of the State's stalwarts (on this occasion).

In the meantime what I have said is true and I am willing to remind our absent-minded friend (not absent-minded in this alone) that I discussed the matter with him during a rather agitated meeting held at his office at the EUR, at the precise time when those events to which I refer in my incidental remark were taking place. I didn't add — because it would have seemed to me most indelicate to mention my interlocutor's opinion (nor did I do so in Senator Gui's case) — the opinion which, on that occasion, was opposed to the opinion I was, as is my habit, objectively sustaining. But so that Senator Taviani, who is willing to deny the reality of my opinion, should not be troubled by the fear that I might suggest he shared my views, I hasten to assert that Taviani's views differed from mine, as do the views of so many today. These, with Taviani at their head, are persuaded that this is the only way to defend the State's authority and power on such occasions. Are they thinking of instances abroad? Or have they been prompted? I, on the other hand, had previously informed the Minister confidentially of the view, which I have now reiterated and amplified, that in cases such as these, cases of actual guerrilla warfare (or anyhow of virtual guerilla warfare), it is not possible to act as in the case of ordinary crimes, although even for these Parliament has unanimously introduced certain reforms it considered overdue from a humanitarian point of view. In the case which concerns us, it is a question of contriving, with all due precaution, to consider the idea of an exchange of political prisoners (an unpalatable but fitting definition) with the object of saving other innocent human lives, of humanely granting a breathing space to opponents even if these are beyond the pale, of achieving a brief suspension of hostilities and to avoid an increase in tension and the loss of the State's power and credibility — since we are involved in an exhausting legalistic duel, burdensome for those implicated and detrimental to the State's efficiency. Thus a whole complex of political motives should be considered and weighed, without, for the moment, adopting too unyielding an attitude which doesn't take into account, even minimally, the humanity and wisdom some of the most civilized nations have shown in painfully similar circumstances and which have led them to adopt that amount of reasonable flexibility Italy refuses to countenance — ignoring the fact that it is assuredly not the strongest State in the world or materially and psychologically equipped to lead the way for countries such as the USSR, Israel and Germany (not however that of Lorenz), casting humanity and wisdom to the winds.

Senator Taviani's unexpected response — which I still fail to comprehend and which, in view of my predicament, I deem inconsiderate and provocative — induces me to give a brief account of this individual who has been a member of the Christian Democratic Party for over thirty years. There is nothing personal in observations which, in the circumstances, appear inevitable. What strikes me — and this is a Christian Democrat weakness that should be eliminated in the current reforms of the Party — is a succession of formal adherences to various minority groups. Taviani, with his sudden, unmotivated and quite astounding right-about turns has been a living example of such an attitude. A Christian Democrat by persuasion, Taviani has joined every minority group in turn, contributing to each his unquestionable efficiency, wide ranging abilities and relative openmindedness. Having myself left the ranks of the *Dorotée* [a powerful minority group of the Christian Democrat centre] after 1968, and having had clear intimations that Taviani was looking to me at this juncture to instil enthusiasm and balance into a group which, despite its divergences, might stabilize the position of the Christian Democratic Party, I waited in vain for an appointment which had been offered me and then for others, until I realized that the stability pursued and achieved was other and quite opposite. Those were the days when Taviani favoured a drift to the right, an alliance with the Socialist Party, as a solution to our political crisis. And we who had heard him advocate for years a quite different policy looked on in amazement — especially since the Christian Democrats had broken off even the most superficial relations with that Party for a long time. But later, inspired by political realism, Taviani became convinced that salvation could only derive from a shift towards the Communist Party. However by the time the last presidential elections took place, Taviani, together with certain other individuals from my party, fearing lest my name be tainted with Communist contamination and although I was as usual out of contention, set up a sort of day-to-day man-hunt against me — vexing on account of its personal connotations and such as to suggest possible American interventions, but furthermore totally pointless since the man they were persecuting was far from being an eager contender for the succession. Throughout the long political career he suddenly abandoned without any plausible reason — except perhaps the chance of claiming higher respon- sibilities — Taviani has filled, among other posts, (after a brief and unsuccessful stint as Party secretary) some of the most varied and responsible in the Ministry. Of these the most notable are those at the Ministry of the Interior and the Ministry of Defence, both held for a long time and involving the complex mechanisms, influential positions and confidential ramifications they afford. It might be mentioned in this context that Admiral Hencke, later Chief of the SID and then of the General Staff for Defence, was one of his men and collaborated with him for many years. The importance and delicacy of the numerous positions he held may account for the influence he has had on the Party and on Italian politics until he appeared to have retired from the scene. Throughout the period he held these two highly confidential positions he had direct and intimate contacts with the United States. Might there perhaps be some American or German significance to his denials?

The letter is delivered to the Press on the afternoon of 10 April. All the papers publish it. Obviously the pleasure of exposing such a dramatic dissension within the Christian Democratic establishment overcomes the scrupulous reserve the Press, inspired by a 'sense of the State', claimed to have adopted. Senator Taviani's brief biography outlined by Moro is greeted with unanimous relish. Of course it is all common knowledge, but coming from Moro it acquires a new significance. Needless to say, those who relish it most are the Red Brigades. In their fifth communiqué which accompanies Moro's letter they write:

> Among the statements the prisoner Moro makes here we under-sign his brief and far from exhaustive assessment of State-Hooligan Emilio Taviani. We make no comment on what Moro writes because, despite his typical contorted jargon which takes the form of veiled allusions even when stating the obvious, he expresses unambiguously his opinion of Taviani, of his machin-ations for power in the Christian Democratic Party, and of the conspiracies he is involved in.

It's true that this letter is very convoluted and veiled, even though it's one of Moro's more freely expressed missives. And free is the right word: Moro begins to free himself, Pirandellically, from for-mality once he has dramatically entered into life. The transitions from stage character to 'solitary man' and from 'solitary man' to human being are those which lead to salvation according to Piran-dello.

This letter reveals moreover an irony the political Moro generally concealed. And he did well to conceal it for few things are harder to understand and more impenetrable than irony. If a man can be hanged for a simple phrase taken out of context, how much more may he be hanged for an ironic phrase. Such as for example '. . . humanely granting a breathing space to opponents even if these are beyond the pale . . .'. Thus Moro wants to grant the Red Brigades a breathing space, to see them as opponents! What more do we need to realize that he has passed over to the Red Brigades? And indeed Senator Taviani informs the papers that he has 'no intention of entering into negotiations with the Red Brigades.'

Whether he has been intimidated or converted, Moro now speaks with and for the Red Brigades — such is the verdict which, like a heavy tomb-stone, descends upon the live, pugnacious, logical man Moro continues to be in the 'People's Prison', while outside the already deceased Moro is remembered and honoured, the Moro to be immortalized as the 'Great Statesman' he never was. Montanelli, in his senile, doting nostalgia for the State (I say this without mockery because I too feel a certain nostalgia for it — except that he believes he once glimpsed such a thing in Italy and I never have), Montanelli intones a 'Requiem for Moro'. And the Communist Antonello Trombadori exclaims in the Chamber of Deputies: 'Moro is dead!' While a group of 'Friends of Moro', self-appointed or selected from among his many 'friends', prepares a monstrous document of misunderstandings: *the Moro who speaks from the 'People's Prison' is not the Moro we knew*.

In fact Moro has never been more true to his character of acute politician than in his letter to Taviani. Taviani's denial has made him bitter, plunged him more deeply into the situation of a 'solitary man', but at the same time it has somehow broadened his scope, given him the chance to manipulate the Red Brigades by surreptitiously sowing seeds of doubt in their midst. Especially in the last sentence, in the question: 'Might there perhaps be some American or German significance to his refutation?' Which could be a simple corollary to Taviani's political biography briefly but rather ruthlessly outlined — and in fact that's what it is: Taviani is America's man just as Hencke was Taviani's. But it isn't hard to imagine the effect of such a question on young Red Brigades recruits — Moro, one of SIM's top men and one of the most intelligent, wonders whether America's man has, once again, in refuting such an obviously true fact, been instructed and commanded by the Americans, and the Germans . . . And if Moro wonders openly and rhetorically, doesn't that imply that he's in fact sure of it? In which case by capturing Moro and keeping him prisoner they have played the game of the Americans and the Germans, unwittingly and unexpectedly served their cause — indeed participated in it.

Had Moro let drop such a hint during the long conversations they certainly had, or during the 'trial', they wouldn't have taken it seriously, but seen it precisely as a hint, an attempt to sow dissension. But Moro addresses this question — this certainty, this accusation — (and what's more in a moment of anger and despair) to his 'friends'. And isn't it rather disturbing to learn that America's man, the 'State Hooligan' Taviani is as keen as their own leaders, as the heads of the Red Brigades, to have Moro remain in the 'People's Prison' and die there?

Maybe all this is no more than a flight of fancy. Yet it's not improbable that Moro's letter was responsible for that kind of dichotomy within the Red Brigades of which it's hard to give any precise indication but which, at a given point became perceptible. Sufficiently perceptible to induce the Italian Socialist Party, although it is part of the governing majority, to disturb the climate of State idolatry by suggesting to the other parties and especially to the Christian Democrats, that negotiations be initiated. Since it's unthinkable that a Party, a whole Party should act on a sudden impulse to seem more humane and sensitive, we can only assume that the Italian Socialist Party — that is, those responsible for disturbing the State-worshipping front — had some intimation of this dichotomy.

Something new and unforeseen is undoubtedly happening within the ranks of the Red Brigades. In the sixth communiqué, delivered to the editorial office in Milan of the daily *La Republica* on 15 April, they announce 'at this point we have made a choice.'

The choice consists in circulating only through clandestine channels any intelligence they have obtained — and thus, in particular, anything revealed in the course of Moro's 'trial' — which they proclaim has been concluded with his death sentence. The reason for this choice is that 'the government Press is always at the service of the class enemy, and that lies and mystification are what it aims for — as it has unequivocally proved in the last few days . . .'. A rather trivial reason that suggests an admission of past errors — belated into the bargain. Besides even if they take it for granted that the official press indulges in mystifications, they can't deny that it has invested the Red Brigades' activities with an almost mythical aura and widely publicized their theoretical and practical communications. And from a realistic point of view, however deceitful and deceiving its interpretations of the Red Brigades' exploits and communications may be, it always reaches an audience already disposed or predisposed to accept them; and the texts published unabridged reach strata of sympathisers which clandestine circulation could not reach. Thus by imparting their decisions and information to the official press the Red Brigades gained more than they lost. Why have they now chosen to be silent?

Is it that, with their highly developed sense of the theatrical, of the unexpected, of suspense, they want to mark time? Do they have to take stock, prepare for action? Or do they feel the need at 'headquarters' of more co-ordination between the ranks, of a tighter control over the ranks? And especially over Moro's jailers? If we consider this hypothesis we might even suppose (suppose, suppose!) that greater co-ordination and control would be required as a consequence of the doubts Moro's attack on Taviani and the unsatisfactory issue of the 'trial' have sown in the minds of the younger recruits, the less experienced elements in the Roman ranks. And the fact that the outcome of the 'trial' has been unsatisfactory can easily be inferred from the sixth communiqué, where they go to great pains to stress that:

> The Christian Democratic Party has no secrets — neither its role as watchdog for the bourgeoisie, nor its duty as pillar of the Multinational State — which have not been revealed to the Nation. What mysteries can the Christian Democrats, from De Gaspari to Moro, conceal which the People haven't already learnt and paid for with their blood? . . . Therefore we have no resounding revelations to make . . .

No secrets, no mysteries, no resounding revelations — since everything was already known, since nothing has been revealed in the 'trial', one might as well have left Moro in via Fani to share the fate of the five murdered lackeys of the SIM.

Even the Red Brigades are well aware of having been inconsistent. And this statement is immediately followed by an amendment: '. . . Aldo Moro's cross-examination has revealed the vile complicities of the regime, identified by name and deed those who are the real and concealed culprits . . .' Inconsistent once again — since this implies that certain things could be revealed, even resoundingly. And if the communiqué is seen as the ratification of a verdict, there is a further and more serious inconsistency — in that Moro emerges, precisely while he is condemned to death, as the 'least implicated of all' (to borrow Pasolini's words), least implicated in the conspiracies for power, in the scandals, in the depravities. In fact more like a witness than a defendant — even a witness for the prosecution: one of those witnesses public prosecutors cultivate and cherish, one who 'identifies', 'indicates', 'lays bare'. There isn't a single item in the report which suggests any positive guilt on his part, any specific responsibility. Nor is it ever stated at any point that he is justly accusing the others to wrongly save himself. So that one is reminded of that incident of the Mexican revolution reported by Martín Luís Guzmán in his great book *The Eagle and the Serpent*, where the revolutionary General, victoriously entering a village, summons five or six notables and enjoins each one to pay a given sum: so many thousand pesos to the first within three hours; twice as much to the second within four hours, and so on, doubling the amount for each and extending the deadline. Failure to comply will be punished by hanging. After three hours the first, who is too poor to pay, is hanged. But all the others, even before the time conceded them is due, hand over the money. Contented, the General extols the success of this system to his adjutant who observes: 'But the first one didn't pay.' And the General: 'He didn't have the means to pay. I was well aware of this. That's precisely how he served my purpose.'

Something rather similar emerges from the sixth communiqué. But what mainly emerges is a note of anxiety, of uncertainty or indecision — even in the terrible decision of the death sentence. And one might suppose (suppose again!) that it was this indecision which provoked the expedient they resorted to in the seventh communiqué — the one the Red Brigades were later to disown as a counterfeit and which the 'official' Press accepted as such, while tactfully hinting at their doubts by putting the word between inverted commas. And here a lot could be said about the mythical rigour and truthfulness with which, together with their deadly accuracy and elusiveness, the Red Brigades were invested by the general public and even, perhaps unconsciously, by such institutions as the police force, the judiciary and the Press. A striking example of which is this incident in a Northern provincial bank: at the cash desk an individual presents himself who, nonchalantly and unobtrusively opening his coat to reveal a gun, asks the cashier to accompany him to the manager's office, adding that he's sent by the Red Brigades. Then, always in the name of the Red Brigades, he requires the manager to hand over eighty million lire. Having pocketed the sum he issues a receipt, asks to be escorted to the door, instructs them to wait until 6 p.m. before giving the alarm (an instruction with which they scrupulously comply) and disappears. A striking example and strikingly comic — but a telling symptom of a reasonably wide-spread state of affairs.

The 'counterfeit' seventh communiqué is delivered late in the morning on 18 April. Graphically it contains elements later adduced as proof of its inauthenticity. Linguistically there is an additional note of mocking cynicism, of gruesome frivolity. Those who wrote the previous communiqués, the unquestionably authentic ones, would have been more solemn and wordier.

> Today, 18 April 1978, ends the dictatorial reign of Christian Democracy which, with the logic of tyranny, has criminally held sway for over thirty years. Simultaneously on this date we announce that President of the Christian Democratic Party, Aldo Moro's execution by 'suicide' has been carried out. We indicate precisely where his body lies so that it may be collected. Aldo Moro's remains are submerged in the muddy depths of Lake Duchessa (that's why he talked of being bemired) 1800 m. alt., approx., at Cartore (RI), on the borderline between Abruzzo and Lazio.
>
> This is only the first in a long sequence of 'suicides' — 'suicide' should not be the sole 'prerogative' of the Baader-Meinhof band.
>
> May the various Cossigas, Andreottis, Tavianis and all those who support the Government begin to quake for their crimes.
>
> P.S. We remind the various Sossis, Barbaros, Corsis, etc., that their liberty is still 'supervised'.

What seems to confirm its authenticity, what leads to the assumption that it does come from the Red Brigades is mainly the fact that, concerned as they have always been with dates, coincidence, symbolic correspondences, could they possibly have let the 18th of April go by without making some gesture, even if only the delivery of a communiqué? For on 18 April 1948 the Christian Democratic Party's great electoral victory had marked the beginning of the regime of the SIM. Could the Red Brigades fail to celebrate in their own way its thirtieth anniversary?

61

Even the communiqué's uncharacteristic tone, its gruesome light-heartedness, could be accounted for by its authenticity. Whoever wrote it knows that Moro is alive; knows he's making a fool of the police, of the SIM. Moreover it isn't until the 20th, in the evening, that the Red Brigades issue the seventh communiqué, the real as opposed to the false seventh communiqué. Why did they wait two days? Obviously so that the effect of their hoax should be fully exposed to the nation — the fruitless, ridiculous dragging of Lake Duchessa. Not to mention the fact that the hoax may well have answered an urgent need for diversion, a decoy. Indeed, on the morning of that same 18 April, the police had discovered a Red Brigades 'hideout' in via Gradoli, not far from via Fani. The diversion of forces from Rome and of attention from any clues the Red Brigades might have left in the via Gradoli flat could well have been a sufficient motivation.

In the 'real' seventh communiqué, which consisted of two paragraphs, the second concerns the 'counterfeit' communiqué: 'The counterfeit communiqué of 18 April', 'the gruesome initiative of psychological warfare experts'. They don't condemn it overmuch nor do they try to explain it. They seem genuinely convinced that psychological warfare experts have suddenly taken up arms against them and that the counterfeit communiqué is the outcome of such expertise. And one might even agree with them if one could imagine for a single minute that the Ministry of the Interior was capable of taking any initiative. In fact the 'counterfeit' communiqué could just as well have been devised by the Red Brigades as by the Government — if you allow that the Government was in a state to devise anything. For it served both parties — and both took advantage of it. As *ballon d'essai*, as dress rehearsal, as a handy means of discharging tensions, emotions and opinions into a fake event — which would eventually be proved fake. So that the real event which would emerge later at a more or less accurately calculated date would be somewhat deflated, somewhat diminished. Moro had been condemned to death — by the Red Brigades directly and indirectly by the Christian Democratic Party. A means had to be found to reduce and deflate the reactions of disapproval, horror and pity the news of his execution would provoke. This was required equally by both parties. Christian Democracy must come to terms with Christianity — of which a pale flicker was vaguely perceptible even among practising Catholics (and more than a flicker among the non-practising and the secular) confronted with the Moro affair. While the Red Brigades must come to terms with that left to the left of the Communist Party which still called them 'comrades' (albeit misguided comrades) and which — since the journalist Casalengo's murder — was not only beginning to distinguish between homicide and revolution, but was also beginning to suspect that the ever-lengthening list of revolutionary crimes might perhaps serve the cause of the revolution but, more surely and immediately, would result in counter-revolution and repression.

So the papers tactfully declare that the 'counterfeit' communiqué was thus defined to arouse the suspicion that, though false as to its contents, its origin is authentic. The Red Brigades refer to it as a 'gruesome initiative', less tactfully turning suspicion into direct accusation — of the regime, the Government and of President of the Cabinet Andreotti. 'A gruesome initiative'! As if — granted that the 'counterfeit' communiqué didn't come from them — the announcement of Moro's death sentence and their intention to carry it out was any less gruesome! To carry it out unless . . . And here in the 'real' communiqué for the first time they state terms which until then had appeared through their contrivance to have been the personal solution advocated by Moro alone. 'We will only consider the release of the prisoner Aldo Moro in relation to the release of Communist prisoners.' This is an ultimatum: the Christian Democratic Party and the Government must give a 'clear and definitive' answer within four hours after 3 p.m. on 20 April.

The 'authentic' or 'second' seventh communiqué (whichever we choose to call it) is immediately followed on the same 20 April by a photograph of Moro delivered to the editorial office of *La Republica* in Milan. As proof of what in bureaucratic jargon is termed 'being alive', he is holding a copy of the previous day's paper. He doesn't seem any the worse for wear — as weary as ever.

The next day Zaccagnini receives another letter from Moro. It states, not without lucidity and convincingly enough, that the 'blind consideration for reasons of State' which precludes the ransoming of his life is tantamount to the re-enforcement of the death penalty in Italian constitutional law.

Dear Zaccagnini,
I appeal to you, and in so doing my intention is to appeal formally and, to a certain extent, officially to Christian Democracy as a whole, which I take the liberty of addressing still in my capacity as President. This is a tragic moment. Doubtless the nation has problems I do not wish to under-estimate, but which can find a reasonable solution, even as regards security, while still maintaining the humane, Christian and democratic ideal with which the most civilized States have complied in similar situations, when confronted with the problem of protecting innocent lives. And in fact, together with the problems of the State there are those which concern my person and my family.

I do not believe that you can disassociate yourself from these terrible, heart-rending problems with the indifference and cynicism you have shown hitherto during my forty days of tribulation and still look history in the face. With profound bitterness and amazement I have seen you adopt, without any serious, humane or political appreciation, an attitude of rigid finality.

I have seen it adopted by those in power without the slightest evidence that a topic of such magnitude has, at any time or place, been discussed.

No dissenting voice — inevitable in a democratic party such as ours — has contrived to surface. Even my own unhappy family has been, as it were, silenced and is unable to raise a desperate cry of affliction and express its need for me. Can you really all agree in wanting my death for a so-called reason of State, which someone treacherously presents to you as a solution to all the nation's problems? Solution to our problems indeed! If this crime is perpetrated a sequence of disasters will follow such as you cannot countenance. You will be swept away. A break with any humanitarian ideals that still survive in this country will follow. Despite your apparent unity a split within the Party will follow which you will be unable to bridge.

I consider the many Christian Democrats who, for years, have identified the Party with my person. I consider my friends in the Party and in parliamentary groups. I consider my numerous personal friends to whom you can never make this tragedy acceptable. Is it possible that at this dramatic hour all these should renounce their right to be heard and to play their part within the Party as they have done in less stringent circumstances.

I plainly declare that for my part I cannot absolve nor justify anyone. I expect the whole Party to prove its basic sincerity and kindness together with that spirit of freedom and humanity which readily and harmoniously emerge in every parliamentary debate on subjects of this order. I address no one in particular but turn to all alike. However, it is to the Christian Democratic Party primarily that the country turns, on account of its reliability, its ability always wisely to reconcile reasons of State with humane and moral reasons. Should it fail now this would be its first failure. It would be swept away by the flood and that would be its end.

Such a terrible event as a death sentence decided by some leader obsessed with problems of security (which can be solved by extradition), I beg you, let it not occur without each one of you having thoroughly weighed all the consequences, sincerely examined his conscience and heeded its dictates. Any opening, any sign of hesitation, anything that reveals a true awareness of the problem's magnitude could be of the greatest significance as time runs out.

Say at once that you refuse to make an immediate, stark reply, a reply that involves death. Dispel at once the image of a party unanimously determined to kill. Remember — and may all the political powers remember — that the Republican Constitution, as a first sign of renewal abolished the death sentence. But you, my dear friends, would thus have it reinstated, without trying in any way to stop it; by your own actions, insensibility and blind concern for reasons of State making it once again part of our constitution. Here, today as in past centuries, in this democratic Italy of 1978, the Italy of the Beccaria, I am sentenced to death. The execution of this sentence depends on you. I ask no more than that my reprieve be granted — that it be granted for none other than the vital reason, of which you Zaccagnini are aware, that my family needs my care, help and guidance.

At this moment my greatest dread is that my family be left unattended — for it cannot be unattended — because of my Party's inability to assume its responsibilities, to act boldly and responsibly at one and the same time.

I appeal to each of my friends individually, those friends who are at the head of the Party, who have worked together with me for years in the interests of the Christian Democratic Party. Remember the sixty crucial days of crisis experienced together with Piccoli, Bartolomei, Galloni and Gaspari under your leadership and with Andreotti's unfailing support. God knows what pains I took then so that all would turn out for the best. I did not think then, as indeed I have never thought, of my personal security or comfort.

The Government has been established, and all the thanks I get for that and for so many other undertakings is the lonely fate of a political prisoner sentenced to death, deprived of my dear ones, without a goodbye, with no fond hands to comfort me. If you do not intercede a chill page will have been written in the history of Italy. My blood will be upon you, upon the Party, upon the Nation.

And you above all, Zaccagnini, you who are mainly responsible, reflect. Remember at this moment — a moment no doubt of excruciating decision for you — your extraordinary insistence and that of the friends you had appointed to that end, your insistence to have me as President of the National Council, to have me party to and co-responsible for the new phase which was about to begin and whose progress would undoubtedly be fraught with difficulty. Remember my energetic resistance mainly for personal motives which you all know. Then I gave in, as always, to the will of the Party. And now here I am at death's door, because I said yes to you and said yes to the Christian Democratic Party. Thus your responsibility is personal in the utmost. Your yes or your no is decisive. But bear in mind that if you remove me from my family you will have done so twice deliberately. This is a burden from which you will never be freed.

May God grant you insight, dear Zaccagnini, and insight to our friends, to whom I address a desperate message. Do not consider the rare occasions when we had no cause to obviate concessions but the many on which we resorted to humanitarian principles and thus, despite unpropitious circumstances acted constructively. If compassion prevails, all is not lost for the country.

Not all the papers publish this letter. And compassion, though it provokes some tremors, does not prevail.

The Christian Democratic Party is, according to the Press, 'lacerated by uncertainty'. Moro's family publicly states a 'resolute' request that the Party 'declare its willingness to accept the conditions for the prisoner's release whatever, in substance, these may be.' The Party, lacerated more by the certainty that it must do nothing than by uncertainty, can only entrust International Charity (a Vatican-sponsored humanitarian society of which hardly anyone has ever heard) with the task of 'seeking possible means of inducing President Moro's kidnappers to set him free'. In fact there are no possible means since the Christian Democratic Party makes a point of re-asserting 'its unfailing dedication to the democratic State, to its institutions and to its laws, in active solidarity with the con-stitutional parties.' But among the constitutional parties the Socialist Party breaks off at this point its *inactive* solidarity. It wants to do something to save Moro's life. Thus it becomes a sort of Prodigal Son, or Black Sheep.

To assuage the Christian Democrats' laceration Paul VI intervenes — a few hours before the Red Brigades' ultimatum expires and by a letter the Vatican radio broadcasts and of which the papers publish an autograph reproduction the next day. A letter with an apparently highly Christian motivation but which, in fact, reveals in its exhortation to 'those of the Red Brigades' to release Moro 'simply, unconditionally' a tacit acceptance — not to say approval — of the Christian Democrats' declared 'unfailing devotion to the State'.

In the 'People's Prison' Moro, unlike the majority of Italians, is not impressed by the Pope's prostrating himself before 'those of the Red Brigades', and well aware of the fact that Paul VI has a stronger 'sense of the State' than the French Minister of the Interior, Prince Poniatowski who, not so long ago, declared that it was perfectly licit to negotiate with terrorists in order to avoid the sacrifice of 'innocent human lives'. In other words, Prince Poniatowski shares Moro's views. And it cannot be said that the French State isn't a State. It is one, and with all the trimmings — perhaps even too many.

So Moro will try to persuade the Pope. 'In actual fact the swapping of prisoners benefits (and this is an argument I humbly beg to submit to the Holy Father) not only those on the other side but also him whose life is at stake, the non-disputant, that is the ordinary citizen like myself.' And in one of his last letters he will observe, less humbly, that the Holy See's attitude to his case denotes a departure from previous attitudes and a refutation of the entire humanitarian tradition: 'This is something atrocious, unworthy of the Holy See . . . I don't know if Poletti [Cardinal Poletti] can rectify this enormity so unlike the Holy See's general attitude . . .' — obviously referring to the Pope's gesture a month before when he offered himself as hostage to the German terrorists who threatened to massacre the passengers of an aeroplane in Mogadishu. An offer which, at the time, had appeared unrealistic — but which stems from the only reality a Pope can invoke and honour when he is the helpless and more or less defeated witness to explosions of violence.

As was to be expected, the appeal to the Pope had no effect whatsoever. And the Christian Democrats' announcement that it has entrusted International Charity with the task of seeking 'possible means' is seen by the Red Brigades as vague and inconclusive (communiqué of 24 April). However the ultimatum is deferred. The position adopted by the Italian Socialist Party is doubtless what prevents the Red Brigades from carrying out the sentence. Maybe at this point the Government might have tried — were it only with contempt, with cynicism — to fan the flame of dissent smouldering in the Red Brigades ranks (between those who would have decided that Moro must die and those who would set him free in exchange for even purely nominal concessions from the Italian State). I repeat, there is no overt sign of such a dissent; but it can be sensed, anticipated. Perhaps because I am trying so hard to understand them too. To understand 'those of the Red Brigades' as the Pope calls them

— even if I don't love them as the Pope claims he does. To understand those who are guarding Moro and judging him — during that trying and dreadful daily intimacy which would inevitably emerge. During the exchanges of words — trivial, grudging, justificatory. During communal meals. During the prisoner's slumber and the jailer's vigil. During their care for the condemned man's health. During their perusal of his missives and the risks incurred whenever these were delivered. So many imperceptible gestures, so many thoughts carelessly expressed but which derive from the innermost recesses of the heart. Eyes that meet when all defences are down. The sudden and unexpected exchange of a smile. Silences . . . All of this, all the minutes day after day — during over fifty days — how could it fail to establish a bond between the jailer and the jailed, the executioner and his victim? Till it becomes impossible for the executioner to be an executioner.

Moro, in a letter dated 29 April writes:

The compassion of him who brought the letter [from his family, published in one of the papers] excluded the accompanying notes referring to my death sentence [by the Christian Democrats in their refusal to negotiate].

This, I would suggest, is the high point — the highly Christian point — of the whole tragedy.

In their eighth communiqué, the Red Brigades stipulate the conditions for Moro's release. They demand the liberation of thirteen individuals — a selection of Red Brigades, proto-Red Brigades and neo-Red Brigades prisoners. The choice is provocative. The delinquency of the proto-Red Brigades men, though at the time of the trial they pleaded social and political motivations, is deemed by general consensus to be unquestionable; and Cristofero Piancone — the only one whose release they try to justify and who is therefore perhaps the most recent recruit — has been in jail for barely two weeks accused, together with accomplices, of the murder of the jailer Cotugno; his crime is thus too recent for the request not to seem provocative. While Curcio and the rest are being tried in Torino and the trial is still under way. In fact it would have been better to have waited, to have postponed it till a more propitious date; but once started it would be even more absurd to free them before or even immediately after the verdict has been pronounced.

But apart from the obvious provocation implicit in the selection, one can't help wondering why they should have chosen the number thirteen. The Red Brigades may not be superstitious but they know the Italians are. Could there be a subtle and gruesome irony in their choice, a suggestion that they know the negotiations will come to nothing and that Moro's unlucky fate is already sealed?

Moreover the feeling increases that the split to which we referred earlier is widening. There is a discrepancy between this communiqué and Moro's letters — which unquestionably take into account the opinions expressed by the men who surround him. These would seem to be prepared to play safe — especially since the Moro they would thus spare is in fact 'already dead to his friends' as the Mafia jargon puts it: politically dead as Montanelli sadly observes and Trombadori proclaims. Whereas the Red Brigades who issue the communiqué appear bent on hardening the Government's heart and obtaining an absolute, final 'no' which would sanction the execution

70

of the verdict.

Already on 19 April the extreme left-wing paper *Lotta Continua* had published an appeal for Moro's release signed not only by representatives of the extreme left (including Dario Fo), but by Bishops, Roman Catholic and lay intellectuals (amongst them Raniero La Valle, a Catholic who had been elected Senator in the Communist Party's electoral roll) and even by two such prominent communists as Umberto Terracini and Lucio Lombardo Radice. But the Red Brigades dismiss this appeal as just another of the many appeals addressed to them by 'certain bourgeois notabilities' and 'religious personalities' (including perhaps the Pope), and invite the signatories to address a similar appeal to the Christian Democrats and to their Government for the release of the thirteen men of the Red Brigades. And it's all right to address such an invitation to the Pope and Bishops, since as we said above, what the Pope requires is no less than the Red Brigades' conversion (with the Pope as Saint Francis and the Red Brigades as the Wolf of Gubbio), without, on the other hand, requiring that the Roman Catholics who govern the State should acknowledge the fact that the preservation of innocent human beings (and such, according to the Pope, is Moro: 'a good and worthy man whom no one can find guilty of any crime or accuse of lacking a social sense or of not respecting justice and peace') is a principle which ought to override all others. Those who represent Christ's Church, and he who supremely represents it, should require no more than what Count Attilio in *I Promessi Sposi* calls an 'impossible dream' — Father Cristoforo's 'humble opinion': that there should be no more threatenings, hired threateners and thrashings.

However when this same invitation is addressed to *Lotta Continua* and the others from the extreme left who signed the appeal, it is less reasonable. For one can't help feeling that they are more or less entitled to warn the Red Brigades, secluded in their ivory tower of ideological and juridical madness, of the terrible mistake they are committing since, at some future date, the State — in one of those bursts of energy which follow defeat and stem from impotence — will require that the price be paid precisely by this section of the left, which, ideologically, is most obviously associated with the Red Brigades.

On 24 April — the very day on which a number of papers receive the eighth communiqué — a further letter from Moro to Zaccagnini is delivered to the Roman Catholic paper *Vita*. In it he repeats with greater urgency what he had said in earlier letters and which is indeed wholly consistent with what he has always maintained: that the Government is the representative of Christian Democracy; that a superior, irrevocable code prescribes that innocent human lives should be spared; that there is 'no political or moral reason' why such a code should not be applied to his own case. Once again Moro's point of view is that of a militant radical Christian Democrat. But in this case the Christian Democrat, who had formally been acquainted with all the dissensions which might occur between factions and individuals, knows nothing of what is now happening within the Party, of all the discussions and conflicts which must surely proliferate on such a momentous occasion:

> We know nothing or next to nothing concerning this affair which is the most important and pregnant with consequences to have involved the Christian Democratic Party for years. We do not know what attitude the Secretary or the President of the Cabinet have assumed — some vague hints from Bodrato of a more or less humanitarian tendency . . .

Moro is right. At that moment a certain unease, a feeling of guilt is beginning to spread within the Party even among those who, though excluded from the select group where indecisive decisions concerning the case come to a head, occupy none the less responsible positions.

But despite the fact that Moro still raises the question and begs for a solution, he is already convinced that nothing will be done to save him. He writes, more as admonishment and warning than as threat:

> The Christian Democratic Party should not imagine that by liquidating Moro the problem will be solved. I shall still be there — an irreducible object of contention and choice — to see that Christian Democracy is not used as it is used today.

And he adds:

> For that reason, because of an obvious incompatibility, I request that neither State authorities nor Party members attend my funeral. I wish to be followed by those few who truly loved me and are therefore worthy of accompanying me with their prayers and their affection.

The Christian Democrat official organ *Il Popolo* prints Moro's letter 'to keep the public informed' and out of an 'indestructible regard' for the old Moro. As to the new Moro, it invokes as attenuating circumstance for his sins of alienation from the State and censure of the Party, the fact that he is kept in 'total darkness' and 'painful constraint'.

This is on 25 April, the day the liberation from Nazi-Fascist rule is celebrated. The flood of rhetoric rises. Resistance against Nazi-Fascist domination — an important factor in the Christian Democratic Party's veneration for Moro — is recalled and transferred to the resistance against negotiating for Moro's life. Unfortunately that same resistance is an important factor for the Red Brigades as well, who see themselves as its heirs, as those who maintain and re-enact it. No one has told them that it wasn't a revolution, nipped in the bud perhaps, but ready to flourish again when the time is ripe, but simply a revival — a revival of pre-Fascist Italy — paradoxically involving the juridical survival of Fascist Italy — where, somehow or other, in a tentative, make-shift way, the new and better theories and practices current throughout the world would be incorporated.

From the Party's head office in Piazza Gesú, Rome, a document is communicated to the papers which I have already qualified as monstrous. Some fifty individuals, 'old friends' of Aldo Moro's, solemnly declare that the man who writes to Zaccagnini, who asks to be delivered from the 'People's Prison' and discusses means for doing so, isn't the man who had been their friend for so long, the man whose 'cultural background, Christian spirit and political vision' had drawn them to him. 'He is not the man we knew whose spiritual, political and juridical vision inspired our participation in the establishment of this Republican Constitution.'

We all know how signatures to manifestos and to public protestations are obtained in Italy, and especially in intellectual circles — frequently over the telephone and with inadequate information as to their purport. How assent is absent-mindedly given on the strength of the ideas or opinions we share with whoever requests them — so that we won't be bothered again. So it's quite possible that some of the signatories acquiesced with a similar absent-mindedness to the protestation concerning Moro ('one or two' as Pirandello would have said). But they shouldn't have done it. This was no public protestation but rather a protest: Moro's bill of conduct hadn't been honoured; or rather the bill of conduct that had been foisted on him.

Remarkable among the signatories of this protest are the names of a well-known philologist and a no less well known Augustinian scholar — who's a Cardinal into the bargain. How is it possible that the philologist doesn't see that the man who writes from the 'People's Prison' is essentially and clearly the same man who wrote *Antigiuridicità nel diritto penale*; who, in 1947, wrote the article reproduced in the March–April 1979 issue of the journal *Studium*; who less than two months ago made the speech in Parliament in defence of Senator Gui? And has the Augustinian scholar forgotten how hard, not to say impossible, it is to know a man? How arrogant, unloving and uncharitable it is to want to assert and assess what he was and what he is. 'I consider wholly correct that rule according to which a friend should be loved neither more nor less than we love ourselves. For if I too am unknown to myself, I am in no way unfair to him when I say that he is unknown to me; especially since, in my opinion, he is also unknown to himself.' Or did the Cardinal, ignoring the precept Saint Augustine followed, love Moro better than himself and thus know the old Moro better than himself?

He knew him not at all. And what is more, he now refuses to try and know him, now when more than ever before he should know him, understand him, stay by him, not abandon this 'lone man' confronted with death, with that dreadful death imposed upon him by other men. 'A bishop', writes Saint Augustine's Cardinal, 'has to enact the truth within his heart: before God in confession, and before many witnesses in his writings.' In this writing, which is his since he signed it, in this repudiation of the man incarcerated in the 'People's Prison', did the Cardinal Archbishop, the Augustinian scholar, really believe that he was enacting the truth within his heart before many witnesses and before the principal witness, Moro? This is a question which bewilders and distresses me — and I'm not one of that shepherd's flock. What then can Moro's bewilderment and distress have been?

74

He says: 'I would not have believed it was possible.' In a letter delivered to a Roman paper on the evening of 27 April and which is worth quoting here in full:

Since my letter published in response to certain ambiguous confused but substantially negative attitudes which the Christian Democratic Party has adopted towards my case, nothing has happened. Not that there was any lack of topics for discussion. There were a great many. On the other hand what the Party, its secretary and its representatives lacked was the moral courage to start a discussion on the topic proposed which is none other than my survival and the means to achieve it practically and realistically. It's true, I am a prisoner and I am not in a happy frame of mind. But I have not been subjected to coercion of any kind, I am not drugged, I write in my usual style, however ungainly this may be, my handwriting is unchanged. Yet it is said that I am *another* and not worthy of being taken seriously. Thus my suggestions are not even answered. And when I make the honourable request that the leaders of the Party or some other constitutional organ should meet, because what is at stake is the life of a man and the fate of his family, you only carry on with your degrading conventicles which reflect your dread of discussion, your dread of the truth, your dread of signing a death warrant with your own names.

But I confess that I was deeply pained (I would not have believed it was possible) by the fact that certain friends, among them Monsignor Zama, Veronese, G. B. Scaglia, without either understanding or imagining my distress — which does not deprive me of lucidity and free will — doubt the authenticity of my contention, as though it were under the Red Brigades dictation that I was writing. Why this certainty of my so-called non-authenticity? Between the Red Brigades and myself there is not the slightest identity of views. Because the fact that I maintained from the start (and, as I have made clear, from way back in the past) that I consider the swapping of political prisoners legitimate, as it has been in wartime, does not constitute an identity of views. And I consider it all the more legitimate when, by not swapping, someone continues to be in serious distress, but alive, and the other is killed. In fact such an exchange benefits (and this is a point I humbly beg to submit to the Holy Father) not only the other side but also him who is not among the contenders, but whose life is at stake, the ordinary citizen like myself.

What makes you suppose that the State would go to rack and ruin if, once in a while, an innocent man survives and, in exchange, another goes into exile instead of going to prison? This is what it all amounts to. It is in this position — which guarantees the death penalty to all those the Red Brigades take prisoner (and there are likely to be no small number) — that the Government has entrenched itself, the Christian Democrats have irretrievably entrenched themselves and all the other Parties have entrenched themselves — the Socialists with some reservations, which should be urgently and positively clarified since there is no time to lose. In such a situation the Socialists might play a decisive part. But when? Woe betide you, my dear Craxi, should your present tactics fail! I want to dwell briefly on this argument, which runs on as my arguments always tend to do. But it cannot be said too often to those stubborn, relentless members of the Christian Democratic Party that exchanges of prisoners have frequently and widely been undertaken in the past in order to save hostages, to spare innocent victims. But it is time to add that not unbeknown to the Christian Democrats, in a reasonable number of cases freedom (with extradition) has been conceded to Palestinians in order to avoid the serious threat of reprisals which might endanger the community. And it should be noted that it was a question of serious and terrible threats but in no way as imminent as those which today confront us. Yet the principle was accepted then. The need to infringe the rules of strict legality (extradition serving as a substitute) was acknowledged. There is reliable evidence that would make all this clear. And let us not forget that by acting thus, as necessity required, these states certainly had no intention of showing disregard for the interests of their allies who, in fact, have maintained friendly, confident relations with them.

Where and by whom has any of this been mentioned in the Christian Democratic Party? It is within the Party that such problems are not bravely confronted. And for me it is a matter of life or death, my death practically ensured by the Christian Democrats who, entrenched behind their questionable principles, do nothing to save a man, whoever he is, but in actual fact one of their more prominent members and long-standing militants, from the scaffold. A man who had ended his career by sincerely renouncing the Presidency of the Government and who was literally dragged by Zaccagnini from a life of pure meditation and study to don the equivocal vestments of Party President for which there was no adequate candidate in the context of Piazza Gesú. I have asked Zaccagnini more than once to assume the role he thrust upon me and for which he is perfectly suited. But he is content to assure the President of the Cabinet that all will be done according to his wishes

And what is to be said of the Onorevole Piccoli who, according to what I have read somewhere, has declared that if I were in his place (that is free and at ease in Piazza Gesú for instance) I would say what he says and not what I say here? If the situation were not, to say the least, so painful, so tragic, I would very much like to see what the Onorevole Piccoli would say in my place. For my part I have declared and demonstrated that I said precisely what I say today on past occasions with complete objectivity. Is it possible that no statutory, formal meeting has been summoned, whatever the result? Is it possible that there is nobody brave enough to require it as I require it in total lucidity? Hundreds of parliamentarians wanted to vote against the Government. And now no one is prepared to tackle a question of conscience? And this with the convenient pretext that I am a prisoner.

You condemn *lagers*, but what regard have you for a prisoner whose bonds are solely material and whose intellect is unimpaired? I ask you, Craxi, is this fair? I ask my Party, I ask all those who were so devoted to me in those happy days is this admissible? If they do not wish to summon any further formal meetings, so be it, but I am entitled to convene the National Council in all urgency for the purpose of discussing means of setting their President free. Having made this decision I delegate as Chairman the Onorevole Ricardo Masassi.

It is public knowledge that my family's present difficulties are the main reason for my struggle against death. With the passage of time, and after many vicissitudes, desires have lapsed and the spirit has been purified. And, despite my many shortcomings, I believe that I have led a moderately generous and modestly considerate life. I shall die, if such is my Party's decree, in the fullness of my Christian faith and in the profound affection for an exemplary family which I love and over which I trust I shall watch from the heavens above. Only yesterday I read the tenderly loving message from my wife, my children, my beloved grandson and the other grandchild I shall never see. The compassion of him who brought the letter excluded the accompanying notes referring to my death sentence — inevitable unless by some miracle the Christian Democrats recover their senses and take things in hand. But this blood-bath augurs no good either for Zaccagnini or Andreotti or Christian Democracy or indeed for the Nation. Each one will bear his responsibility.

I repeat, I do not wish to be surrounded by those in power. I wish to have beside me those who have truly loved me and will continue to do so and to pray for me. If all this is decreed, may God's will be done. But let none of those responsible seek to hide behind the call of an imaginary duty. All things will come to light, soon they will come to light.

So many things in this letter are significant, so many need clarifying. And deciphering. But first let us consider the words: '. . . when by not swapping someone continues to be in serious distress, but alive, and the other is killed'. *Someone* (*Taluno*): 'a pronoun indicating quality; to be used correctly where it is a matter of stressing the quality of one or more people; but as a rule not many.' (Once again Tommaseo: I write these pages on the Moro affair submerged under a flood of newspaper cuttings and with Tommaseo's dictionary in their midst, firm as a rock.) Undoubtedly Moro wants to draw the recipient's attention to the quality of the person or persons to be released by the State — and thus that it could negotiate on the number and perhaps release less than the thirteen stipulated by the Red Brigades. An interpretation confirmed by the words: '. . . the State would go to rack and ruin if, once in a while, one innocent man survives and, in exchange, another goes into exile instead of going to prison?' Someone has become one — there is no possible doubt. Especially as he adds: 'That's what it all amounts to', as though to imply: *a single person, have you understood?* And it might even be legitimate to infer that the 'other' isn't yet in prison, but about to go there.

Thus the Red Brigades, or at least those in charge of Moro, have chosen him as mediator for eventual negotiations and informed him of the minimum price — actual or symbolic — which they require from the State. Moro makes this more or less explicit. Yet those who ought to understand fail to do so. Henceforth we have reached the 31 and 47, or what in the Sicilian code for the game of lotto corresponds

78

to 'the dead man speaks'. Speaks in the dreams and nightmares of his 'friends'. And is still speaking.

But so much else might be significant. From Moro's warning to Craxi and the Socialist Party — which might involve more than an endeavour to save his life — to his insistence on appointing Masassi to preside over the National Council of Christian Democrats — Masassi whose name had not previously figured in the news among those who, in the Party's confidential meetings, had expressed themselves in favour of negotiations. And, unless it was a case of almost uncanny intuition, someone must have informed Moro. A disturbing hypothesis this, which we shall leave, as Moro left it, to disturb his 'friends'. And then there is that 'I have read somewhere' to be noted as proof of what I called the Red Brigades' 'prison ethics' — that he was given the daily paper (perhaps more than one) to read. Or they may have acted as a sort of press agency, providing him with cuttings according to a variable criterion of what they wanted him to know. But the fact is that he was informed. And by saying that the notes referring to his death sentence had been excluded and only the letter from his children, printed in the daily *Il Giorno* on 26 April, delivered to him seems to suggest that till then they had given him the papers uncensored.

And finally here for the first time he writes the word 'power' in all its terrible simplicity — a word he sees at last in all its true, profound and corrupt reality. 'I do not wish to be surrounded by those in power.' For in the previous letter he had mentioned the 'State authorities', the 'men of the Party'. Only now has he found the right epithet, the dreadful word.

He had lived for power and by power up to nine o'clock on the morning of 16 March. He had hoped to possess it still — perhaps so as to assume it again fully, certainly so as to avoid *that* death. But now he knows it is the others who possess it. And in the others he perceives its ugly, idiotic, cruel countenance. In his 'friends', his followers of those happy days — those gruesome, obscene, happy days of power.

'Those happy days', the happy days of power. With irony. A distanced irony, bitter and painful.

He doesn't seem to have ever enjoyed power. He loved it but he wasn't happy with it. To be the best among *others*, to be in a position to despise them, gave him perhaps a Christian appreciation of his own triviality. And that was what distinguished him from the *others*. That was why he was singled out from among the others — and to a certain extent by the others — for death.

In the story of his life — that story which is already 'literature' (and which here we are only trying to interpret) — there are, from the very beginning, premonitory signs. We have only to glance at *Moro* by Corrado Pizzinelli published in 1969 — a biography written for a series entitled *Famous Men*, full of gossip and intended as gossip. There are points the journalist seems to savour as though they were omens (which indeed is what they are in the eyes of those who read it today!). This is how he describes Moro, the Minister of Justice:

> As Keeper of the Seals all his weaknesses are exposed. He is over-pedantic, fastidious, slow and finical. And what is his main preoccupation? Would you believe it? Prisons and prisoners, which he visits extensively. . . . His incursions into the Italian social underworld are incessant and thorough. We would like to ask a psychoanalyst what might be the secret motivations for this strange attraction prisons and prisoners exert over a man who, let us not forget, is devoted to ties and tie-knots.

Isn't the journalist's association of prison visits to ties and tie-knots (or hanging) rather disturbing? And then, referring to the period when Moro presided over moderate left-wing governments: 'Beginning at the time of Kennedy's death', this period actually ended in June 1968 with the other Kennedy's assassination. 'Strange coincidence: it's in the gap between these two tragedies that Moro was in power.' And again: 'The word fatality recurs frequently in his vocabulary . . .'

But let's turn from coincidences to the events which involve them. After Moro's letter of 27 April — the last he addressed to the Christian Democratic Party and the Italian politicians (unless others have been withheld from the public) — Moro's family entrusts the papers with a resolute message:

> After many days of anguish and suspense Aldo Moro's family addresses an urgent appeal to the Christian Democratic Party to have the courage to assume responsibility for its President's release. This family considers the Christian Democratic Party's attitude wholly inadequate for the safeguard of Aldo Moro's life.
>
> May the Christian Democratic Commission know, may the Onorevoli Zaccagnini, Piccoli, Bartolomei, Galloni and Gaspari know that with their unyielding stance and their rejection of every initiative derived from various quarters they are ratifying Aldo Moro's death sentence. If these five gentlemen do not wish to assume the responsibility of declaring that they are prepared to negotiate, let them at least convene the National Council of Christian Democrats as its President has formally requested.
>
> Our conscience can no longer keep silent before the Christian Democratic Party's attitude. We believe that, by this appeal, we are also expressing our relative's will. He himself is unable to express it without being declared practically insane by almost all the Italian political body, and first of all by the Christian Democrats and associated groups of Aldo Moro's so-called 'friends' and 'acquaintances'.
>
> If you want to avoid a long period of sorrow and mourning there is no point in denying the bitter truth. Instead it is necessary to face it with lucid courage.

The Government replies after two days with a memorandum written, according to the papers 'by the hand of Andreotti'. And this too requires perhaps a psychoanalyst's attention — the fact that the papers cling to this detail of Andreotti writing 'by hand' the Government's message. The image of a man writing a sentence. It is possibly this focus on a physical detail which started the unconscious process of responsibility-shifting which sooner or later will be exposed (and if sooner it will mark the end of the Andreotti Government).

The Government memorandum says:

The request transmitted by the Christian Democrats to the Government thoroughly to examine the implications of the humanitarian solution outlined by the Italian Socialist Party will be considered at a meeting of the International Commission for Security to be held shortly. Let it be noted here and now that the Government's decision not to consider even the slightest abrogation of the laws of the State is public knowledge. Neither can it overlook its moral obligation to honour the sufferings of those families which mourn the tragic consequences of the terrorists' crime.

If this memorandum was truly written by Andreotti, by his own hand, he wrote it more in Moro's style than his own. He is usually clearer, more tritely clear. What coincidence will we perceive later in this fact? In the meantime let us translate: 'The Christian Democratic Party asks the Christian Democratic Government to make the Socialist Party keep quiet (since the Government's quiet depends on their keeping quiet) by showing a certain interest in a humanitarian solution to the Moro affair. The Government has understood and will play the game. There will be a select ministerial meeting which will be quite pointless since the Government has already made up its mind not to negotiate on any account with the Red Brigades, out of consideration for those families whose relatives were killed by the Red Brigades.'

Moravia is right: in Italy it's the family which accounts for everything, justifies everything, is everything. As Lincoln said of democracy: from the family, for the family, to the family. And therefore, to outshine the Moro family's rights, to extinguish them — since insofar as it is a family it has rights — what could be better than to serve up a collection of families already mourning their kin, or at least the families of the five men of Moro's escort? A further, freer translation of the memorandum, and a more realistic one, might read: 'An otherwise impotent Government can only manifest its power and somewhat minimize the censure and resentment its impotence provokes by allowing the Red Brigades to proceed with its *egalitarian* solution to the Moro affair. If then, in reply to the Holy Father's prayers, the Unnamed who rules over them happens to be touched by Grace as was Manzoni's Unnamed, the Government can only say that it will be delighted by the fact that the Onorevole Moro has been restored to his family.'

On the first of May the papers announce that further letters from Moro have reached President of the Republic Leone, President of the Senate Fanfani, President of the Chamber of Deputies Ingrao and President of the Christian Democratic Parliamentary Group Piccoli (now replacing Moro as President of the Party). And it would seem that by addressing himself to all these Presidents, these Top Men in the Government, Moro wants somehow to consummate his task, his duty — to himself, to his family — but henceforth without much hope.

He has also sent a letter to Masassi and one to the Secretary of the Socialist Party, Craxi.

Only two out of these seven letters have been made public. The letter to Craxi is published by the recipient; and the letter to Leone was, apparently, delivered to a press agency.

Moro has so little hope left, he knows so well that he has, as he says to Craxi, 'a minimal respite', that in his brief and formal letter to Leone he indulges in a note of irony (but perhaps the formality itself is somewhat ironic): 'May the many forms of solidarity attempted direct you on to the right path.' Among the forms of solidarity Leone attempted was the one which was to let him down two months later and thus force him to resign. And it's perhaps more precisely to this one Moro is referring — the Communist Party.

On 5 May the Red Brigades' ninth communiqué is delivered to the Press. Apart from the usual indictments of the SIM, the Christian Democrats, the assassins 'headed by Andreotti', Berlinguer and the Berlinguerists, it contains exaggerated or even gratuitous polemics against Craxi and the Socialist Party. Which leads one to suspect that 'Headquarters' may have felt the need to promote these polemics for 'internal use' as it were, against the 'fringe'. As a warning and reprimand to those who might have wanted to go on negotiating for 'less than thirteen' — that is those who require from the State a less mortifying price than the release of thirteen Red Brigades men.

Moreover such a suspicion could give rise to another — that the Red Brigades might be inclined to 'disqualify' the Socialist Party's electoral potential — in the by-elections due in a week's time. A disqualification diligently conducted by those papers the Red Brigades define as 'Governmental'. (Headlines: 'Craxi has changed sides', 'The Socialists are isolated', 'Craxi's initative is deflated', 'Craxi is forced to toe the Christian Democratic line'.) And this suspicion is worth considering.

The communiqué ends on the terrible announcement: 'Thus we conclude the battle started on 16 March by carrying out the verdict to which Aldo Moro was condemned.'

'Carrying out'. Present gerundive of the verb to carry out. An *extendable* present. And it was more convenient to extend it towards the future, towards hope. 'All our attention', writes the editor of the Christian Democratic paper *Il Popolo*, 'is focused on the gerundive.' It's a moot question whether focusing on a gerundive has ever saved or can ever save a man's life — but by now we are in the realm of surrealism. The gerundive, filled with hope, rises like a balloon — it floats between heads of Parties, newspaper editors, the radio, television, popular opinion. Not the present gerundive of the verb to carry out, but the term gerundive. One third at least of Italy's population is wondering what the hell this gerundive can be on which hope for Moro's life is suspended. Is it a special police corps, specially trained and equipped for actions of exceptional danger and precision? Or is it the name of someone who has some influence on the Red Brigade?

Aldo Moro's life and death — his life or his death — have become unreal. Their only reality is in the gerundive. They are nothing more than a present gerundive.

There's a postscript to the Red Brigades' ninth communiqué, the gerundive one:

Any evidence that has emerged from Aldo Moro's interrogation and any information we have obtained, as well as a comprehensive politico–military account of the battle which ends here will be supplied to the Revolutionary Movement and to the C.C.C. [Organization of Militant Communists] through clandestine channels of propaganda.

This is an admission of defeat.

The decision, already foreshadowed in the sixth communiqué, to entrust only clandestine publications with the evidence from Moro's trial, assumes in this communiqué which leaves no doubt as to the execution of his sentence, an air of more obvious and sinister duplicity — an attempt to conceal defeat. In the third communiqué they had said: 'Nothing must be concealed from the public and such is our custom.' They had repeated it, more forcefully, in the fifth communiqué. In the sixth, although they had already opted for the clandestine media, they vaguely promised that 'everything will be made public'. But in the ninth the promise appears to have been forgotten. Has any evidence emerged from Moro's trial or has it not? And more importantly, is there still a public from whom 'nothing must be concealed'?

Both questions should perhaps be answered in the negative. Moro's interrogation has yielded nothing sensational, nothing that can serve as indictment. And the decision to kill him has clearly had the unconscious effect of consolidating their feeling of exclusion, of isolation, or an ever increasing constriction within that cell which henceforth has only underground exits, secret passages — which, when the time comes, will be blocked — and not by them.

We recall the relish with which they published Moro's attack on Taviani and how satisfied they must have been by the fear and bewilderment it provoked in the spheres of Christian Democratic power. And how they gloated over Moro's remark concerning Andreotti ('. . . he perceives how his crony Andreotti, in particular, will do his best to turn the affair that concerns him into a "bargain" [Moro's own words] as he has always done throughout his career'). Had they possessed any further revelations made by Moro, any other assessments, were they likely to refrain from making them public? What would be the point?

The fact is that Moro still sees the Party that accuses him of no longer being himself, that repudiates and disowns him, the Party temporarily perverted by exterior promptings ('Someone is spitefully prompting you') as his own Christian Democracy — pliable, accessible, yielding but also tenacious, patient and prehensile; a kind of octopus capable of tenderly embracing dissent and regurgitating it well chewed, as assent. A Christian Democracy which comes from far and will go far — comes from as far and will go as far as that Roman Catholicism, inherent in the natural Italian constitution, has still to go. He still says 'My Party' even when it is least disposed to include him, when he senses that — more than the Red Brigades — it is sentencing him to death: 'I shall die if such is my Party's decision . . .'. Beyond Zaccagnini, Andreotti, Piccoli there is still the Party — 'irreplaceable basis' of the government — which can't fail to recognize its mistakes, to recover the reason for its existence and its survival, and for which the *Moro affair* will one day be 'an incomprehensible moment of litigation and dissent'.

There are of course inconsistencies and contradictions (even oversights and errors) in the letters we know — and probably many more in those we don't. But how could it be otherwise considering the suddenness of the change in his circumstances — from the summit of power to total impotence (as in Calderon's *La vida es sueño*) — as well as all he has to put up with from the enemy at hand and from his distant 'friends'? Yet we can't fail to perceive true consistency in his non-consent to the trial, his rejection of it for himself and for Christian Democracy — just as, a few months earlier, he had rejected the trial of Deputy Gui insofar as he was a Christian Democrat with whom Christian Democracy as a whole identified and by whom it stood firm. And — quite consistently — he blames the Christian Democratic Party, can neither politically justify nor humanely forgive it precisely for not standing firm by him, for not identifying with him as prisoner of the Red Brigades and accused by them. And he doesn't even blame the Party as a whole, Christian Democracy in its essence, its nature and its destiny, but only those members of the Party, those Top Men who have assumed the right to decide.

And maybe some 'evidence' did emerge and will come to light. But it will be too late because we can no longer ignore the possibility of skilful manipulations of tapes or text. Moro was faithful to *his* Christian Democracy. In other words, while we, now, try to loosen what Pasolini called 'an enigmatic bond', he didn't entirely free himself from it. He loosened it before God when, stripped of his power, he perceived the diabolical nature of power. He didn't loosen it before the citizens of the Italian Republic.

On the morning of 9 May Professor Franco Tritto, a friend of the Moro family, receives a phone call (and this isn't the first) from the Red Brigades. The call, having been taped by the police, is published in the papers and broadcast two months later on the remote chance that someone might identify the voice — and goodness knows how many mythomaniacs did identify it and how many rascals tried to besmirch some enemy or friend!

Member of the Red Brigades: Hello. Is that Professor Franco Tritto?
Franco Tritto: Who's there?
MRB: Doctor Nicolai.
FT: Nicolai who?
MRB: Are you Professor Franco Tritto?
FT: Yes I am.
MRB: Indeed, I thought I recognized your voice . . . Look here, despite the fact that your phone is tapped, we'd like you to bear a last message to the family.
FT: Yes. But I want to know who's speaking.
MRB: Red Brigades. Got it?
FT: Yes.
MRB: Well, I can't stay long on the phone. So this is what you must tell the family — go in person, even if your phone is tapped never mind, you should go in person and say this: we're carrying out the President's last wishes by informing his family where Onorevole Moro's remains are to be found. Right?
FT: But what should I do?
MRB: Can you hear me?
FT: No. Please say it again.
MRB: No, I can't say it again, look here . . . So you must tell the family that they'll find the Onorevole Aldo Moro's remains in via Caetani, which is the second turning to the right off via delle Botteghe Oscure. Right?

FT: Yes.

MRB: There they'll find a red Renault 4. The first figures on the number plate are N.5.

FT: N.5? I'll have to phone. (He is overcome with tears.)

MRB: No. You should go in person.

FT: I can't . . .

MRB: You can't? You should make an effort . . .

FT: Yes. Of course. Yes . . .

MRB: I'm sorry. I mean if you phone it won't . . . it won't detract from the President's wishes being carried out as he expressly asked us . . .

FT: Talk to my father, please . . . (He can't speak for crying.)

MRB: All right.

Tritto Senior: Hello. What is it?

MRB: You'll have to go to the Onerevole Moro's family or send your son or else phone them.

TS: Yes.

MRB: Just do that. Your son has the message. Right?

TS: Can't I go myself?

MRB: You can go yourself.

TS: Because my son isn't well.

MRB: You can go yourself. That's fine, of course. So long as you do it quickly, because the Onorevole Moro's wishes, his last wishes were that we should inform his family, because his family has to recover the body . . . Right? Goodbye.

We've quoted this conversation in full because it raises some significant questions. First, the length of the phone call. What with Tritto's bewilderment, his tears, his passing the phone to his father and the messenger's hesitations and repetitions at least three minutes. In his surprise and distress Tritto behaves, quite unintentionally, as if he wanted to gain time and assist the police. Since the call was made from Termini Station where there's a police station and, presumably, there must always be motorised patrols at the ready connected by radio to police headquarters, it oughtn't to have been impossible to catch the caller before he'd finished speaking. The same remark applies to the messenger. He knows Tritto's phone is tapped and that any delay could be fatal. Yet he remains patient, meticulous and even considerate throughout. He repeats, indulges in an 'I'm sorry', in fact extends to over three minutes a communication he could have made in thirty seconds. This could be accounted for by the fact that he knows from long experience how remarkably slow the police's reactions tend to be (indeed 'the first blue and white police car arrives wailing in via Caetani at 13.20'). But since in this case the news is so sensational and since they've had nearly two months to improve their methods, there's always the risk that an unprecedentedly prompt operation might be launched. What then retains the messenger at that phone if not the *carrying out* of a duty incurred in the service of an ideology but which has now become a mission of humane compassion? Although the voice remains cold the words, the hesitations betray compassion. And respect. Four times he refers to Moro as 'Onorevole' and twice as 'the President'. I doubt if the Italians, in their overt or unconscious anti-parliamentarianism (not entirely gratuitous, not entirely unjustified), had ever realized that the title 'Onorevole' derives from 'onore' until they heard it pronounced by this Red Brigades spokesman together with the name of Moro.

Perhaps that young Red Brigades' recruit still believes we can live for hate and against compassion. But that day, *carrying out* that duty, compassion entered his being as a traitor penetrates a fort. May it finally overpower him!

If one wanted to analyse the Moro affair while disposing of no more than the facts broadcast by the media, it would be necessary, besides separating the little gold from much dross, to take into account that self-denigrating — or self-denigratingly indulged — tendency to see ourselves as incurably inexact, unpunctual and inefficient. Precision, punctuality and efficiency are qualities the Italians in general consider totally foreign to their nature. When an establishment doesn't work, a hospital neglects its patients or has no vacancies, a train is late, a plane doesn't take off, a letter fails to arrive or a festival is a flop, the immediate reaction is always 'Made in Italy'. But there's at least one thing 'Made in Italy' that works — and it's precisely the one which is now our home-product *par excellence*. And I agree that it's nothing to boast about and that one home-product that works doesn't preclude our exclaiming 'Made in Italy' for all those which don't. But it's a fact that it works and that we are therefore not doomed by nature or bad luck to inexactitude, unpunctuality and inefficiency.

The Red Brigades function to perfection. Yet (the yet is inevitable) it's Italian. It's 'Made in Italy', whatever links it may have with foreign revolutionary sects or secret societies. Not that we want to suggest here any connections — unless they be fortuitous and purely individual — with another more ancient and certainly more tried home-product — but similarities indisputably exist between the two: the Red Brigades have probably studied every available textbook written on guerrilla warfare, but in its organization and its activities there is something which undoubtedly derives from the Mafia's unwritten textbook. Something 'domestic' even in its precision and efficiency. Something more easily identified as an appropriation of Mafia tactics than as conforming to revolutionary laws.

Thus laming, for instance, is an appropriation of the laming of cattle practised by the rural Mafia. Thus too their method for obtaining connivance and soliciting protection or complicity — a method where corruption plays a very small part, where open threats are not to be discounted but where the main factor is the suggestion that no double-dealing or collaboration with the authorities escapes their notice; the method, in other words, of spreading a mistrust of public authority, of making the invisible presence of the Mafia (or of the Red Brigades) more immanent and fearful than that of the visible police force. And thus too the ruthless persecution of prison wardens which procures, inside the prison, the preferential treatment of revolutionary prisoners as it has always procured that of Mafia prisoners. (But we should not suppose the Mafia instituted this practice only for the sake of comfort — long before it was adopted by political prisoners, the Mafia had seen the prison as a site for propaganda, enrolment and schooling.) But apart from such more or less objective similarities, the public has become aware of a further analogy — that just as the Mafia relies upon and participates in the administration of power — a certain way of administering power — so too do the Red Brigades. Whence the public's apparent indifference, which in fact is the detached attention of spectators who know the play, are seeing a new production they follow without the excitement of wondering *how it's all going to end* and are only interested in noting certain changes in the staging and the actors' interpretation. And one often hears, especially in Sicily, the comment that this Red Brigades business is just *another old story like Giuliano's* — referring to the general acquiescence and complicity of the public authorities, with which the Sicilians were familiar even before it emerged as evidence (evidence, indeed, in this case) in the notorious Viterbo affair. An attitude which might be censured if one ignored the circumstances — but which Trilussa justifies in that couplet which says that nobody relies any more on the church bell since they know who rings it.

Personally I must be and want to be more cautious, and restrict myself to these two points: first that the Red Brigades' efficiency is Italian and strikingly similar to another better known and more widespread efficiency. Second that the Red Brigades' influence isn't eradicated from the Italian political context where it plays an as yet indeterminate and ambiguous part — not, presumably, indeterminate or ambiguous for those who wield it. It would be madness to see the Red Brigades as representative of that independent self-governing revolutionary integrity persuaded it can move the masses and explode all the political structures that restrain them. And it would be a more serious form of madness if they were to see themselves in such a light. Their purpose, function and 'exploits' consist exclusively in shifting relations of power — of the powers that be. And, it must be added, in shifting them minimally. Shifting them perhaps according to that principle of 'changing everything to change nothing' which Lampedusa's Prince saw as a constant in the history of Sicily, and which can be seen today as a constant in the history of Italy. An exercise of pure power, in fact, which can only occur in that inter-party realm where, sheltered from ideological tempests, power now resides. Not that we want to deny that the essence of the Red Brigades is indeed madness. But when method begins to emerge from madness it is time to be wary. Like Polonius with Hamlet. But he wasn't wary enough — and may it not be so with us. For it is precisely in the Moro affair that method begins to emerge.

It has generally been said, and is still said, that the Red Brigades' madness isn't without method. But it's with the Moro affair and through Moro's letters that its purpose becomes gradually clearer. A prisoner and sentenced to death, Moro, like Polonius, found and then followed that thread of method in what must at first have seemed a labyrinth of madness. And already in his first letter to Zaccagnini he seems to have grasped the end of that thread when he says that the Communist Party 'cannot forget that my tragic abduction occurred as we were on our way to the cabinet to consecrate the Government I had taken such pains to establish.' And in the second: 'The Government has been established and this is all the thanks I get . . . Remember at this moment — a moment no doubt of excruciating decision for you — your extraordinary insistence and that of the friends you had appointed to that end, your insistence on having me as President of the National Council [of the Party], to have me party to and co-responsible for the new phase that was about to begin and whose progress would undoubtedly be fraught with difficulty.' And it should be noted that at the same time as he realizes how atrociously he has been rewarded by the Government he has taken such pains to establish, he tends to distance himself from that undertaking, that 'new phase' of which he is not the 'creator' but 'party to', not reponsible for but 'co-responsible'.

The basis of the whole tragedy, what made Moro's death inevitable as a sign of gratitude — of 'thanks' — was the fact that he was instrumental in the Communist Party's inclusion, after thirty years, in the Governmental majority. And the Red Brigades, not content with their explicit reference to this in their communiqués, illustrate it with gruesome daring, impressively and symbolically, when they leave Moro's remains in via Caetani, half-way between via delle Botteghe Oscure, where the Italian Communist Party has its headquarters, and Piazza del Gesú where the Christian Democrats have theirs. (The impact of names: the dark shops, the Jesus of the Jesuits; I don't know whether via Caetani is named after the family of Boniface VIII or that of the Arabist, but in either case it would be equally apt.)

But if the Red Brigades' declared and re-iterated aim is to halt the process of engagement, the union which is occurring between the Communist and Christian Democratic Parties, how is it they don't see that their activities are producing the contrary effect, that through their activities the process acquires an aspect of necessity and urgency? And in the meantime it is for them and against them that the Communist Party is able to go ahead with its invention of the State (and I say invention in the sense in which one says *invention of the Cross* — here again the impact of words: for this one — invention — recalls Saint Helen the mother of Constantine). And it might be said that such an invention, though it was instrumental in preventing Moro's release and in causing the extreme left some concern, and the more 'liberal' and more independent intellectuals some discomfort, did nothing to diminish the Red Brigades' power or hinder any of their undertakings. But one never can tell. It might still be their undoing when the time is ripe. Furthermore on the first day of Moro's abduction, on the evening of 16 March, the impact of this abduction — contrary to the Red Brigades' declared intentions — was already clearly visible (and would be even more so when the sentence was carried out) in the countless red flags flanking, in sympathy and support, the Christian Democrat's white one in the main squares of every Italian city.

Should we then infer from this seemingly blinkered attitude that the Red Brigades' essence and future is really in the realm of 'madness', to put it bluntly or, to put it less bluntly and more astutely, in the realm of an aestheticism for which to die for the revolution now implies to die with the revolution?

Exactly a month after what the Red Brigades call the end of the battle (and even those who don't enjoy battles will breathe more freely when they read an account of a real battle, because one can't help a feeling of suffocation when the term is applied to the murder, with a silenced pistol, in some garage or cellar, of an unarmed man), photocopies of four letters from Moro are delivered anonymously to the editorial office of a little-known weekly. This weekly — *O.P.* (*Political Observer*) — prints them in the issue of 13 June as previously unpublished, although the letter addressed to Zaccagnini had already appeared in certain papers on 30 April. Each photocopy bears the stamp of Roman Police Headquarters certifying its conformity to the original. Who, at Roman Police Headquarters, wanted these letters to be made public?

But even though one of those as yet unpublished is of the utmost interest, few papers reproduce it or mention its existence. Is this because there is now a tendency to dismiss the 'affair', to forget it, or, indeed, because of the interest this letter can't fail to arouse?

The letter is addressed to Moro's wife and presumably written between 27–30 April.

My dearest Noretta,
even if the contents of your letter to the *Giorno* had no positive results (nor did I think it would) it did me a world of good, giving me in my distress the confirmation of a love which remains unwavering in all of you and which accompanies me and will accompany me in my Calvary. To all, therefore, my most heartfelt embrace, my fondest affection.

I am sorry, Dearest, to have given you this additional bother and worry, but I believe that you too, even in your discouragement, would not have forgiven me if I had not required of you what was perhaps a useless act of love, but an act of love none the less.

And now, even at this extremity, I must give you some instructions concerning your delicate task. You should avail yourself of the prudent assistance of Rana and Guerzoni. I see that the Parliamentary groups have kept silent, and amongst them some of our best friends — presumably overcome, as has so often been the case, by the fear of disrupting a fictitious unanimity. What is amazing is that, in no time at all, the Government has seen fit to assess the significance and the implications of such an important event and has opted, in haste and without due thought, for a relentless attitude from which it has not budged — when all that was required was an exchange of prisoners, which is the norm in all wars (and this is, in fact, a war) together with the banishment of those they have released, from the National Territory. It makes no sense to apply the rules of common law. And such rigour in so disorganized a country as Italy! Appearances have been saved, but tomorrow those who have any decency will be sorry for this crime — and the Christian Democrats most of all. Most conspicuous just now is the silence of my friends. You should appeal to Cervoni, Rosato, Dell'Andro and the rest whom Rana knows and urge them to dissociate themselves from the majority. That is the one thing our leaders dread. Otherwise they don't care about anything. Their dissociation must be considered and decisive. They don't realize what disasters will follow this state of affairs and that anything would be better, or at least less bad than this. They must act promptly because time is running out. It might be a good thing to make it known through some statement who (if any) had been persuaded. We need public as well as private support. In all this let Guerzoni advise you.

I was distressed to see in the *Giorno*'s editorial a reference to the *Osservatore Romano* (Levi) by the inevitable Zizola. In substance: No, to the blackmailers. Thus through the medium of this Mister Levi, the Holy See, quite inconsistent with its former attitude, rejects its long humanitarian tradition by condemning now me and tomorrow innocent children to become the victims of this refusal to negotiate. This is terrible, unworthy of the Holy See. Since banishment from the State is common practice in so many countries and even in the Soviet Union, one can't see why here it should be replaced by State slaughter. I don't know whether Politti could rectify this terrible mistake so contrary to the Holy See's normal conduct. This is a theory which serves as an excuse for the worst Communist intolerance and in the name of Communist solidarity. The confusion of tongues has reached an incredible pitch. Obviously I cannot avoid dwelling on the malice of all those Christian Democrats who wished upon me against my will an office which, if it served the Party, should have been preserved for me by accepting an exchange of prisoners which would, I am persuaded, have been the wisest course. Thus in my last hour I am left with a profound bitterness at heart. Was no one prepared to take an independent stand? Giovanni will have to be told what it is that political activity involves. Did no one regret having urged me to take this step for which I was clearly unwilling? And Zaccagnini? How can he remain quietly at his post? And Cossiga who was incapable of assisting me? My blood will be upon them. But it is not of this I want to talk but of you whom I love and will always love, of the gratitude I owe you, of the inexpressible joy you gave me during my life, of the child I took such pleasure in watching and whom I shall watch till the last, I hope. If only I had your hands to hold, your photographs, your embraces. The Christian Democrats (and Levi of the *Osservatore*) deprive me even of these. What disasters will follow on this disaster?

I kiss you, I hug you, dearest Noretta, and you, do likewise to the family and with equal courage. Did Anna really turn up? May God bless her. I kiss you,

Aldo

'State slaughter'. Is it possible Moro wrote this phrase without recalling its precise implications — its reference, that is, to the event or events for which it was first coined and addressed as indictment (an indictment which has become valid even in the currency of those who were least convinced) against certain government organizations and against himself? Most emphatically not. Were it only because one of the articles of the Red Brigades indictment against him refers to it explicitly (first communiqué: 'When the filthy plot will be entirely uncovered Moro, like a good "second" worthy of the part, will bury the whole thing and reward its authors with an avalanche of silence'). Thus in the 'People's Prison' he would have been constantly reminded of the 'State slaughter' and have constantly declared that he had had nothing to do with it. Or that he was the 'least implicated of all' — and only concerning the silence. So he didn't write the phrase unintentionally — but appropriating it, adapting it to his case, expressing it as his own opinion. And then: 'This is a theory which serves as an excuse for the worst Communist intolerance and in the name of Communist solidarity. The confusion of tongues has reached an incredible pitch.'

I have already said that this is a detective story . . . after seven years I can't recall the details of my plot, but here is the broad outline to which the gaps in my memory have reduced (or refined) it. There's an inexplicable murder in the first pages, a slow investigation in the middle ones, a solution in the last. Then, once the mystery has been solved, there is a lengthy revision which contains the sentence: 'Everybody believed that the two chess players had met by chance.' From this sentence it becomes clear that the solution is the wrong one. The perplexed reader re-reads the misleading chapters and finds *another* solution, the right one.

—J. L. Borges, *Ficciones*

Parliamentary Commission of Inquiry into the via Fani crime, the kidnapping and murder of Aldo Moro, the policy and objectives pursued by the terrorists.
Minority report presented by Deputy Leonardo Sciascia

The Parliamentary Commission of Inquiry into the crime in via Fani, the kidnapping and murder of Aldo Moro and the policy and objectives pursued by the terrorists couldn't fail to proceed slowly and tentatively in the first stages, which were concerned mainly with the Moro affair. For it involved forty members and a Chairman who, in fact, was twice replaced, the last substitution — that of Senator Valiante — occurring when a substantial amount of evidence had already been obtained of which he had to take cognisance. The fact that the attendance was reduced to an average of half to two-thirds of the members did little to facilitate the proceedings which were always over lengthy and partly repetitive. To this can be added the implicit and sometimes explicit hostility between its members which reflected that between the different parties of the so-called Constitutional Arch — notably between Communists and Christian Democrats on the one hand and Socialists on the other — during Moro's imprisonment and up to the imprisonment and release of Judge d'Urso — involving, that is, the Socialists' 'humanitarian' attitude which favoured negotiations with the terrorists within the limits of acceptable concessions, and the 'unrelenting' attitude of the Communists, Christian Democrats and others who favoured unmitigated intransigence.

These attitudes were reflected in the Commission's attempts to prove, on the one hand, that a minimum of concessions, resulting from negotiations with the Red Brigades, might have saved Aldo Moro's life (as later the closing of Asinara prison and the intercessions by members of Parliament on behalf of imprisoned Red Brigades members was believed — though not by all and not by us

— to have saved the life of Judge D'Urso); and, on the other, that the Socialists' readiness to negotiate, besides splitting a 'national solidarity' based on intransigence, not only could in no way have saved Moro's life, but furthermore, by advocating personal, private contacts with the Red Brigades and encounters between Socialist militants and militants of the Roman Autonomy considered to be possible intermediaries (which indeed they could have been, as it later emerged,) represented a serious breach of the law, since the investigating magistrates were not informed. Such hostilities (of which there is ample evidence in the Commission's minutes), even if never expressed as clearly as we have done here, were, we believe, a serious obstacle to the Commission's progress and wasted much precious time. For instance the pointless sessions devoted to the Rossellini–Radio 'Città futura' affair: had Rossellini broadcast news of the occurrences in via Fani at least an hour before they took place? If this could be proved it would mean that Rossellini was 'involved' and in consequence his contacts with the Socialists automatically became highly suspicious. But Rossellini couldn't have broadcast the news. At most, since he appears to have studied the Red Brigades' aims and attitudes, he might have mentioned the kidnapping as a possibility.

Anyhow, the question whether Moro might or might not have been saved by negotiations appears gratuitous and irrelevant after so many lengthy sessions, so many pages of minutes. Gratuitous and irrelevant, that is, for the purpose of a Parliamentary Commission of Inquiry. But neither gratuitous nor irrelevant for an inquest between and within the ranks of the Red Brigades and directed by them. Since they were able to decide whether to release Moro rather than to kill him. And the decision to kill him, the dissent to which it gave rise, sparked off the crisis which is leading to their disintegration and annihilation.

It seems to us, on the other hand, that the basic, the vital question which it is the Commission's duty to answer is this: *How is it that the forces the State provides for the protection, security and safeguard of its individual citizens, collectivities and institutions failed to rescue Moro throughout the fifty-five days of his captivity?*

Obviously, and inevitably, time was also wasted seeking to answer the question proposed in item a) article I of the Act establishing the Commission: Had any information been received which had any possible relation to the crime in via Fani, or to

100

eventual terrorist activities in the period preceding Moro's abduction; and if so how was such information checked and exploited? This question gave rise to inextricable myths, memory lapses and time distortions (including the Rossellini–Radio 'Città futura' affair).

And no less pointless were the commission's efforts to answer question b) of the Act: Had Aldo Moro received during the months preceding his abduction any threats or warnings aimed at making him abandon his political activities? Since it's legitimate to assume that every prominent political personality receives such messages, anonymously or otherwise, in the form of warnings or threats, Aldo Moro, whose often unintelligible intentions could easily lead to misunderstandings, was more likely than most to have received — and did in fact receive — some. But even the warning (or threat) he received, presumably while in a 'friendly' country, and from a prominent personality of that country, can't, we believe, be related to his murder — were it only for the fact that it occurred. For such things as we all know are done and not said — indeed not saying them is a necessary condition for their being done. On the other hand it was eminently predictable — in view of their desire to attack the 'multinational State', the democratic and capitalist system at its core and in its leaders — that the Red Brigades should attempt to capture and eliminate a man such as Moro, at the head of Christian Democracy and on the point, so it was rumoured, of extending its alliance and making it thus more flexible, attractive and securely established (and simultaneously making its opponents less attractive and less secure). But the organizations whose duty it was to foresee that the Red Brigades had, in their somewhat rigid and simplistic way, summed up the situation which could lead to Aldo Moro's capture and/or murder, were very far from doing anything of the kind — let alone preventing it.

Thus the question proferred at item c) of the Act: Were the measures for the protection and security of Aldo Moro subsequently proved to have been inadequate or non-existent? can be answered in the affirmative: they were not only non-existent, but furthermore the Commission's attempts to prove it were met with denials so categorical as to be incredible. And it is mainly the character of Police Inspector Leonardi, captain of Moro's escort, such as it emerges from various accounts we have obtained, which deprives them of all credibility.

Thus Savasta, formerly of the Red Brigades, assessing Moro's escort at the University says:

> I noticed three men, one of them elderly . . . Three stood out, amongst them this elderly man who was the most able because he circulated in the crowd . . . Yes, it was Police Inspector Leonardi who circulated more widely than the rest, because a vast crowd had gathered to attend Aldo Moro's lectures. In spite of this he was able to keep everything under control. I was struck by this particular aspect which also helped me to see what sort of an escort it was, whether it was a purely formal escort or a real one . . . Police Inspector Leonardi's attitude was that of a real escort, very much on the alert. It was the sort of escort we were no longer used to. There's a sure way of summing up such things: in the first place their hands were always on their guns; and then their way of mingling with the crowd. There was something different. When an escort is purely formal the men just don't look about much; when it's real you can tell at once, from the way they observe the crowd, how they watch the comings and goings. This seemed to be a real escort . . .

So the Red Brigades had been able to infer from their observations that most escorts were purely formal; and they were surprised to see that, albeit only in a given place, Aldo Moro's escort was a genuine one. But this was entirely due to that elderly man, 'the most able,' who managed 'to keep everything under control'.

And this view of his unequalled competence was shared by General Ferrara:

> Leonardi was an excellent non-commissioned officer — austere, serious, very distinguished, physically imposing, always self-confident; he was brave and never unprepared, a fine shot, top grade . . .

Such opinions lead us to trust all the testimonies concerning Inspector Leonardi's anxiety about Moro's (and his own) safety. More especially his wife's testimony. Leonardi had asked the Ministry of the Interior for other men — either in addition, or to replace those he had and who didn't seem to him to be 'adequately prepared for the service they had to undertake'. This request which Mrs Leonardi dates at around the end of 1977 or the beginning of 1978, has been impossible to trace, either among the documents or in the memory of those who should have received it. And yet he can't have failed to make it. For at that time precisely we know that the Red Brigades were watching Moro and his escort's habits and behaviour closely. And this wouldn't have escaped Leonardi's notice. His anxiety increased as certain signs led him to suspect that the danger was imminent. He had noticed, moreover, that he was being followed and had mentioned it to his wife, specifying to other witnesses that it was a white 128 that followed him.

Towards the end he was so anxious, tense, under-weight, and felt so insecure that his wife describes him as 'no longer himself'. And according to her he would go nearly every afternoon when he came off duty 'and confer with General Ferrara, always concerning his duties'. But General Ferrara categorically denies this, backing his denial with the precise memory of a single such meeting with Leonardi on 26 January which had nothing to do with his duties.

With whom then did Leonardi confer? To whom did he make his report? That he did so Mrs Leonardi is 'a hundred per cent certain'. But General Ferrara, while admitting that Leonardi 'had contacts with all the appropriate channels', asserts that 'Police Inspector Leonardi never sent any report to any one . . . We have made inquiries at all the appropriate headquarters of the capital to find out if Leonardi ever referred to them even orally: nothing has emerged . . . No request either for staff or for reinforcements of men or equipment was ever forwarded.' Which, we repeat, is incredible. Leonardi may not have conferred with the General, but he certainly did confer with someone from one of the 'appropriate headquarters of the capital'. That all trace should have vanished and that it should be denied is an extremely disturbing fact.

When speaking of her husband, Corporal Ricci's widow evokes a strikingly similar picture of nervousness and dread. He never spoke much about his duties at home, but since he'd been appointed chauffeur he was voluble on the subject of the 130 he had to drive ('it was always breaking down') and couldn't wait for the armoured 130 to arrive. Towards the end of 1977 he told his wife it was finally due to arrive, which suggests that it had been requested and promised. But it never turned up. Whence, perhaps, a more marked nervousness around the month of February ('he seemed worried and behaved oddly'). This, coinciding with Police Inspector Leonardi's attitude, shows that they shared a similar anxiety, perceived the same signs. But as in the case of Leonardi, nobody knows anything about a request for an armoured car. Indeed, the Commission was told that had there been any such request it could easily have been satisfied. But why, if it had not been requested, was it expected and, at a given point, not expected any more?

Thus at the University Moro's escort was a real escort but elsewhere, owing to the inefficiency and unreliability of the equipment, it became a purely formal escort. A fact which certainly didn't escape the Red Brigades' notice.

To say today that a more reliable armoured car for Moro, another with good brakes for the escort, efficient arms and both expertise and promptness in handling them wouldn't have been enough to deter the Red Brigades or ensure the failure of their plan, is as pointless as to say that they would have been enough. In undertakings such as Moro's abduction, success or failure may depend on the functioning or not of a minute detail. None the less, malfunction presupposes responsibilities which have to be checked and identified. Yet in its inquiry into responsibilities — which are always individual even if they are extensible and interlinked — the Commission invariably gave up just too soon at the very point of discovering them, of proving them — hindered as it was by formalities, by obstacles within and without.

Item d) of the Act which set up the Commission of Inquiry stipulates an examination of 'what were the eventual malfunctions and omissions with their related responsibilities, which occurred in the administration and execution of the inquest, as regards both the seeking and liberation of Moro and the subsequent murder of the same; and in the co-ordination of the organisms and equipment involved in this inquest.' However the evidence obtained on the subject is so vast that we must extract the main or significant features giving special prominence to some which seemed unimportant, and ignoring others which have been given undue prominence.

For instance, the operations conducted by the police during the fifty-five days between Moro's abduction and his assassination have been widely reported as 'an impressive effort' worthy of the highest praise. And it was indeed an impressive effort: 72,460 road blocks, of which 6,296 in the capital's urban centre; 37,702 house searches, 6,933 in Rome; 6,413,713 individuals checked, 167,409 in Rome; 3,383,123 vehicles checked, 96,527 in Rome; 150 persons arrested; 400 detained. These operations involved 13,000 policemen daily, 4,300 in Rome alone. An impressive effort yet by no means praiseworthy.

These operations, carried out for the most part 'at random' (and thus, as we shall see, with careless omissions), were either useless or misguided. One had the impression — later confirmed — that they were aimed at dazzling the public with their frequency and dimensions irrespective of the results they might achieve. And indeed this was the immediate option, the principle (paradoxically consistent in its actual inconsistency) which was spontaneously adopted. And we have only to recall that order circulated by the head of UCIGOS [Central Office for General Investigations and Special Operations] just after Moro's abduction to carry out 'Plan Zero'. Now 'Plan Zero' was only operative in the province of Sassari; however the head of UCIGOS, who had been Chief Constable in Sassari, thought it was operative all over Italy. There ensued an exchange of frantic phone-calls between police headquarters until it finally emerged that the plan was non-operative. But the point isn't the mistake and its comical consequences; the point is that it was possible to suppose that the carrying out of a 'Plan Zero' in all the provinces of Italy could have any effect whatsoever. What was the use of setting up road blocks or checking vehicles and individuals on the morning of 16 March in Trapani or Aosta? None at all. Except to provide a show of 'impressive efforts'.

Thus every effort was directed — intentionally or not — towards the spectacular, trusting perhaps in the law of probabilities — which didn't work. And it's obvious that in the pursuit of such effects less impressive but more productive measures were neglected; measures which would have given the inquest a less spectacular but more productive appearance. So much so that the Commission was told by the man who was Chief Constable in Rome at the time that he had lacked the men necessary for a shadowing job which wouldn't have required more than a dozen individuals, while in Rome alone 4,300 policemen were making a great show of busying themselves to no purpose. But we shall return to this point. In the mean time let us note that our views on the futility of these operations is shared by Doctor Pascalino, Attorney General in Rome, who declared: '. . . the operations carried out in those days were more for show than for the purpose of investigating.' And it's undeniable that those who decided, who accepted, and who did nothing to direct the course of events more efficiently must be considered — insofar as responsibilities were incumbent upon them — wholly responsible.

Oddly enough, together with these purely formal activities the police force showed a degree of readiness and efficiency which has not been fully appreciated. This is obvious in their identification of suspected members of the Red Brigades which was effected in a matter of days after the events in via Fani, thanks to the publication of photographs in the Press and on television. Twenty-two individuals were identified of whom, however, two had, it later emerged, been previously detained and one was officially residing in France; moreover a fourth was duly registered at the hotel where she was staying. Such blunders — easily accounted for by the endemic lack of communication between services in this country — caused the public to overlook the positive aspect of these identifications: in other words the fact that the police was right in eighteen cases.

Doctor Importà, a police official, justly vindicated the wholly unacknowledged efficiency and promptness of the Roman police on this occasion. The nation wasn't unprepared since after barely three days Roman police headquarters was able to identify eighteen terrorists — anticipating proved and confessed evidence — some of them members of the via Fani group; and since it knew which were the more active elements in the extra-parliamentary sphere (and was even acquainted with their ideological, strategical and practical characteristics). The general opinion voiced by officials and politicians that the State was unprepared for such an attack cannot be accepted without demur. The fact that the Red Brigades' *Risoluzione*, and other texts published by their theoreticians and supporters, had not been properly studied by the police and security forces wasn't necessarily responsible for their bewilderment and confusion or for the blunders, omissions and fruitless operations during the fifty-five days of Moro's detention.

A normal, run-of-the-mill professionalism would have been enough. Even without an acquaintance with these texts (which might have helped to prevent rather than to confront such an event), the police had the advantage of an approximate knowledge of the nature and purpose of the terrorist group called the Red Brigades. They had already been able to identify a considerable number of its members. They were adequately informed as to the protective network on which the group could rely. If the via Fani kidnapping had had a purely lucrative purpose and been perpetrated by a totally unknown, obscure and improvised gang the disadvantages would have been infinitely greater. But the fact is that such advantages were put to no use.

However, let us proceed chronologically and deal specifically with instances where malfunction and omission (and, as ever, the 'related responsibilities') are most blatantly obvious. On the afternoon of the 16th — the day Aldo Moro was kidnapped and his escort murdered — the Fiat 132 in which he was taken away was found in via Lucinio Calvo. In other words, the Red Brigades were able to venture forth, brazenly and unmolested, in this most conspicuous of cars in the very neighbourhood where the crime had just been committed. This mocking gesture — proof that the Red Brigades circulated confidently in that neighbourhood — should have awakened the suspicion that they dwelt there, and supervision ought to have been intensified in consequence. But that's not what happened; and two more of the cars employed in the operation were found in the same street on the 17th and 19th. Considerable risks must have been incurred rather foolishly, it would seem, by the Red Brigades — but they obviously knew what they were doing and how safe they were.

In the mean time, on 17 March, Franco Moreno, who seemed to be seriously implicated in the affair, was arrested — a rather ill-advised measure, perhaps, even if the investigations had only concerned the murder, but totally incomprehensible when they also involved Moro's abduction. Since at the time Moreno, according to the investigators, was the only *identified* member of the group, his arrest, apart from cutting off a potential lead to the site where Aldo Moro was detained, might further prove fatal to the latter's chances of survival. But once again the need for display probably prevailed over professionalism and diligent investigation. However the implications which appeared — and according to the files still appear — to have been serious, somehow dissolved under interrogation and, three days later, Moreno was released.

In the meantime, on the 18th (third of the fifty-five days) the police, in the course of their random house to house searches, came to a flat in via Gradoli occupied by a certain engineer Borghi, later identified as Mario Moretti. They came — but went no further than the closed door. Thus, incidentally, however purely formal the operations may have been, they did take place; yet according both to instinct and to professional common sense a closed door, a door-bell nobody answers, ought to be more significant than one that opens at the first knock; especially since Doctor Infelisi, the magistrate in charge of the inquest, had given instructions that, when confronted with a locked flat, the alternatives were either to await the occupant's return or to break in. Instructions which were obeyed in a number of cases to the discomfort of many an innocent citizen. But in this (to our knowledge) unique case they were not carried out, when they could have been rich in consequences. Apparently the neighbours' assurance that the flat was occupied by decent, unobtrusive people was sufficient to persuade the police official to desist from inspecting it — whereas such an assurance ought to have increased his suspicions since, indeed, the Red Brigades were most unlikely to have done anything to attract attention when occupying a small flat in an overcrowded building.

Exactly a month later, on 18 April, the flat in via Gradoli, registered by the police as occupied by respectable persons, is fortuitously revealed to have been a Red Brigades' hide-out. But the name Gradoli had already figured in the inquest (in vain), owing to a séance held near Bologna on 2 April. And let it surprise no one that a séance should figure prominently in a Parliamentary Commission of Investigation, as in some regional comedy. For twelve 'reliable' witnesses who were, moreover, scholarly citizens of scholarly Bologna, gave evidence before the Commission regarding the séance they had attended whence the name Gradoli emerged. Not one of them claimed to be either an expert or a believer in such practices. They all stressed the 'playful' atmosphere established around the 'planchette' and other accessories to the performance on that tedious afternoon in the country, when they had resorted to 'spiritualism' as a way of passing the time. Yet in the report to the Commission not only did everyone appear to believe that the 'planchette' was automatically propelled, they must actually have believed it since the next day it was reported to DIGOS [Department of General Investigations and Special Operations] of Bologna and later to Doctor Cavina, head of Onorevole Zaccagnini's Press Agency. One name had clearly emerged from the 'planchette's' stutterings: Gradoli. And since there's a village of that name in the province of Viterbo, the police went there in force, presumably to perform the usual random investigations. Obviously to no purpose. Mrs Moro's suggestion that a via Gradoli be sought in Rome wasn't taken into consideration. In fact she was told that there was no such street in the yellow pages of the Telephone Directory. That is to say, no one had taken the trouble to look for that street in the yellow pages, since it's there.

The flat in via Gradoli rented by the pseudonymous Borghi was finally broken into, by pure chance, at 9.47 a.m. on 18 April — not to arrest terrorists but to repair a burst mains pipe. Incidentally it seems that a kind of hydraulic fate pursued the Red Brigades, for the mains in via Gradoli are not the first to have led to the discovery of a hide-out. And since we have mentioned spirits and could also mention clairvoyants in this affair, why not mention fate as well?

The Fire Brigade was of course the first to arrive in via Gradoli. Realizing at once that this was a terrorist hide-out the officer in charge reported the fact. And now further confusion and mystery arise: the Press are on the premises before the police; the *Carabinieri* only hear of the discovery because they happen to intercept a police radio-communication; the Investigating Magistrate, Infelisi, learns the news two hours later and not from the police but from the *Carabinieri*. Judge Infelisi had to give orders for the confiscation of all documents found in the flat, to make it possible for the *Carabinieri* to have a look at them too (though Chief Constable De Francesco denies having forbidden the *Carabinieri* to look at the documents and declares that he knew nothing of the confiscation ordered by the judge — a contradiction which has never been cleared). Nor was there any attempt to take fingerprints or make a prompt and detailed inventory of the contents of the flat — which according to Doctor Infelisi provided no clues as to Moro's whereabouts. However he did feel the need to add: '. . . at least as regards what was brought to my attention', thus admitting the possibility that there might have been items of the contents which were not brought to his attention.

All in all, what occurred between 18 March and 18 April concerning the flat in via Gradoli has an air of improbability, of incredibility; what with spirits (which, according to a letter from the Onorevole Tina Anselmi to the Commission appear to have been much better informed than emerges from the reports of those who attended the séance); providential floods (Providence having perhaps been assisted through carelessness or volition by the hand of man); and a lack of the most elementary professionalism, co-ordination and intelligence.

But there are other incidents worthy of note: we won't dwell on the incident of lake Duchessa — where, doubting the communiqué's authenticity and wasting valuable time trying to establish its authentic-inauthenticity or inauthentic-authenticity, the police behaved as if it were authentic and consequently diverted and dispersed their forces — but concentrate instead on the case of the Triaca Printing Office.

Information concerning individuals involved with the Printing Office and therefore suspected of having links with the Red Brigades, first reached UCIGOS [Central Office for General Investigations and Special Operations] on the 28 March. But a month elapsed before it was in a position to make a report to DIGOS [Department of General Investigations and Special Operations] on the 29 April. This delay was mainly due we believe to what Doctor Fariello of UCIGOS calls 'intermittent shadowing' — that is, shadowing suspects discontinuously so that they won't realize they're being shadowed; which amounts to not shadowing them at all, since chance alone can crown such shadowing with success. Indeed visits to hide-outs, clandestine encounters and all that concerns conspiracies and crimes are not regulated by habit or timetables; neither does a suspect's awareness of being followed depend on the follower's persistence but on his incompetence.

So a month goes by — with Moro still incarcerated in the 'People's Prison' — before the information (which has been somewhat substantiated — sheer good luck having unexpectedly favoured 'intermittent shadowing') — is transmitted from UCIGOS to DIGOS.

On 1 May information concerning the Triaca Printing Office in via Foa is available. The same day DIGOS requests permission to control their telephone communications, and a week later permission to search the premises. The search was to have taken place on the 9th, the day Moro's body is handed over by the Red Brigades. Consequently it is postponed till the 17th. And here we agree with Doctor Fariello when he says that it would have been better to postpone it further: now that Moro is dead a non-intermittent, uninterrupted and diligent supervision of the premises would have yielded no less than the capture of Moretti. But both the head of UCIGOS and Chief Constable De Francesco admit that they had to rush the operation to satisfy public opinion.

The simultaneously belated and premature operation revealed something which can only be described as incredible: in the Printing Office there was a printing press that had belonged to RUS [Army Special Unit Group] and a photocopying machine from the Ministry of Transport. Nothing has been found to account for the photocopying machine's transit from the Ministry of Transport to the Red

Brigades printing office — which may give some idea of the difficulties encountered by the Commission and elicit some indulgence from Parliament and public opinion (or that section of it which isn't overawed by purely formal operations and is able to draw its own conclusions). As regards the printing press, some explanation did emerge, but which doesn't account convincingly for the journey from RUS — which is in fact a branch of SISMI [Military Information and Security Service], that is of the secret services which bear these initials since SID [Defence Information Service] was dissolved — to the Triaca Printing Office. Even admitting that Government offices are in the habit of selling as scrap-iron equipment which, acquired for next to nothing by private persons, miraculously recovers its former efficiency, that this equipment should end up in the hands of the Red Brigades is really a bit much and deserves to be seriously investigated.

And a further incident to be noted concerning the 'malfunction and omissions with their related responsibilities which occurred in the administration and execution of the investigation', is the failure to follow what would have been a major lead to the identification and capture of certain terrorists and, most likely, to Aldo Moro's place of detention. It's now possible to infer this from hindsight; but the police could and should have done so at the time.

According to De Francesco, Chief Constable in Rome at the time, and whose views are shared by Doctor Importa, then head of the Political Department:

> In our investigations, even before Moro's abduction, priority was always given to the *Autonomia* [an extra-parliamentary movement of the 1970s which totally rejects traditional institutions and identifies political crises with individual circumstances], since I believed and still believe that this was the capital's most threatening sector . . . As regards the *Autonomia* I stressed from the start, that is from 16 March, that it was in my opinion the sector where certain elements of the Red Brigades might have found invaluable assistance.

Yet it's hard to see quite how he gave it 'priority', how he 'stressed' it, since no one had been delegated to shadow the leaders of the movement despite the fact that they were all identified. We now know what, at the time, the Chief Constable was only able, on the basis of his beliefs, to suspect: that contacts existed between at least two Red Brigades militants and the main exponents of the Roman *Autonomia*, contacts which were maintained throughout the fifty-five days and after. Indeed meetings actually occurred. A careful shadowing — not intermittent — of Piperno and Pace would have led to the identification of Morucci and Faranda, the two terrorists who had taken part in the events at via Fani and who, in all probability, visited Moro's 'prison' and certainly met up with his jailers. But members of the Commission who asked why the police hadn't taken any such elementary measures as to keep an eye on the leaders of the *Autonomia* were told by De Francesco that he lacked the necessary men. Yet he had 4000 men engaged in purely formal operations!

To this brief list of blunders and omissions can be added the incident reported by the Customs Official Commandant on the 16th, shortly after the events in via Fani:

A man standing in via Sorelle Marchisio noticed two individuals — one of them thinner, about 1m.70 to 1m.75 in height wearing a pilot's outfit, the other shorter, well-built, tougher, with a thick beard. The first was supporting the other by the arm, grasping him firmly above the elbow. They came out of via Pinetta Sacchetti where it joins via Montiglio; they went some way down via Sorelle Marchisio, reached via Marconi and turned towards via Cogoleto . . . There's a surgery there.

The information was immediately transmitted to DIGOS, but the order to search the surgery only reached the Customs Office 'some weeks later'. Yet everything leads one to suspect that what the anonymous witness saw must have been related to the events which had just taken place in via Fani.

One wonders what the motive can have been for such inconsistency and delay, for so many professional blunders. The answer could be lack of preparation for terrorist attacks, and especially for one as remarkable in its method, object and purpose as that of via Fani. But this isn't convincing as an explanation. We've seen that it was possible to identify at once a certain number of terrorists, some of whom we now know took part in the action, and that the sectors of complicity or of more or less reliable support were explicitly noted. Indeed, a more general, unacknowledged lack of preparation is admissible for crimes committed by groups which enjoy on the one hand protection through the public's silence and fear, and on the other through actual or imagined connections with the powers that be. But this can't account for the whole thing. In the Moro affair another explanation must be sought — political, psychological, psychoanalytical.

Undoubtedly the blunders which were made — and which prevented more positive and intelligent measures from being taken — were partly dictated by the conditioning of the media (not of public opinion — public opinion when it exists is less spineless, less willing to accept whatever is on offer, more capable, in fact, of being critical and selective): purely formal operations as, from his 'exalted position' (as Machiavelli would say) Doctor Pascalino described them — but did nothing to put a stop to them. Such operations which, we repeat, in order to be conspicuous, to impress, had to employ vast numbers of men and equipment, precluded the implementation of necessary, basic operations, of constant, diligent and prompt investigations. Not to mention (that is mentioning it none the less) that on the one occasion when, by pure chance, formal operations might have had some result, they were not forthcoming: in front of the locked door of the via Gradoli flat on 18 March.

In our opinion, however, the major obstacle, the most persistently disruptive factor derived from the decision to declare that Moro, the prisoner of the Red Brigades, was no longer Moro the shrewd, thoughtful politician, careful and selective in his choices who, until 8.55 a.m. on 16 March was acknowledged — now almost unanimously if more or less posthumously as in an obituary — to have been. From that moment Moro was not himself, had become another. And as proof one was referred to the letters where he asked to be ransomed, and precisely to the fact that he asked to be ransomed.

We've used the apparently vague but substantially exact word *decision*. Whether this decision was spontaneous or willed, unpremeditated or gradually reached, by a few or by many, it was unquestionably a decision — by the simple fact that it could have been otherwise. And we are well aware that it's impossible to prove that such a decision — never officially stated — may have affected the ways and means of the investigation, constricted them in one way or another. We are moreover ready to admit that the results may not have been conscious and deliberate — not, that is, due to bad faith. But we can't ignore the fact (we've only to read the papers of the time) that a climate had been established, an atmosphere, a state of mind which unobtrusively compelled everybody (with the odd exception) to believe that the *old Moro* was more or less dead and that to find the *new Moro* alive would be no better than finding him dead in the boot of a Renault. To excuse the contents of his letters there was mention, in the early days, of coercion, torture, drugs. But when Moro kept persistently stressing his lucidity and independence of mind ('as much lucidity at least as a man can have who finds himself for a fortnight in exceptional circumstances who has no one to comfort him and who knows what awaits him . . .'), the pitiful image of an altered Moro was presented to the public, a new Moro, a Moro who was no longer himself— to the extent of thinking he was lucid and independent when he was neither.

As a matter of fact this new Moro was asking for those same measures to be taken to save his life which the old Moro, in the course of his political and Governmental career had taken and approved, contravening the laws of the State in order to maintain the peace of the nation: '. . . not once, but on various occasions, a number of arrested and even condemned Palestinians have been released by various means so as to avoid reprisals which could have occurred if they had been kept any longer in prison . . .'. Similar means, unbeknown to the public, had been tacitly (obviously) accepted by the Government, by the governing parties, by Parliament. Was Moro to be told that in his case they would have to be resorted to anything but tacitly — indeed with inevitable publicity and consequent loss of credibility? It seemed preferable to invalidate and refute his arguments from a clinical rather than a political point of view, explain them away as the product of a prisoner's deranged mind. Whence the investigators' lack of interest in his letters.

Onorevole Cossiga, then Minister of the Interior, denies categorically that any attempt was made to decipher Moro's letters: 'No deciphering was carried out during his captivity. The methods employed were unscientific. On the other hand messages from the Red Brigades were subjected to linguistic analyses . . .' What these unscientific methods must have been, and the outcome of the linguistic analyses, could already be perceived at the time. But the same Cossiga, after stating that 'conflicting and even painful opinions' could be voiced concerning Moro's letters, finally admits they prove that

Moro, with his lucidity, intelligence and logic had understood

114

what those who were bargaining with him really wanted: to be acknowledged as a Party which, although outside the State, is within Society, and with which a dialectical relationship is possible.

Precisely. And Moro, without departing from his basic convictions (which Cossiga adequately summed up — as did Moro himself in his lectures on the State), couldn't do otherwise than play the game so as to gain time and give the police a chance to find him. There seems to be no reason why Moro, intelligent and astute as he was, should have behaved like a fool. Since he had a chance to gain time and to communicate with the outside world, how could he not take advantage of these favourable circumstances? And although he only mentions his hopes concerning an exchange of prisoners, one can only assume that, in all probability, he had others — that he believed the police would finally discover the site where he was incarcerated.

Thus he would have tried to give some clue as to where he was — unobtrusively, of course, and in code. Anyone would have tried. Yet such a desire and the ability to fulfil it were injuriously denied him, when he — an expert in the craft of words, inclined to use them over-ambiguously at times — more than anyone else, would have known how to conceal meanings among words (as Pirandello would have put it).

Thus the ciphers contained in his messages might have been sought in the incorrect use of certain terms, in the apparent carelessnesses. When Cossiga and Zaccagnini, wishing to describe the conditions in which Moro finds himself, quote a passage from one of his letters (the one addressed to Cossiga, Minister of the Interior): 'I am under the full and unchecked control of my captors', it's odd they should have failed to notice that the passage contains an incongruity and doesn't define exactly the kind of control to which Moro is subjected. For what does 'unchecked' signify? Who could and should check the Red Brigades? Thus the interpretation which has been suggested seems most convincing (especially after the revelations of former Red Brigades members): 'I'm in a fully inhabited building which the police haven't yet checked'. And possibly even the word 'under' might contain a topographical clue. But besides failing to decipher, no attention was accorded to what was obvious — as, for instance, the 'here' in the sentence: 'it should be possible to summon Ambassador Cottafavi here', probably slipped through the self-censorship Moro scrupulously observed as a rule, as well as through the Red Brigades censorship, and which should be read: 'in Rome'. And this was by no means an insignficant clue, considering the time wasted seeking him outside Rome.

In fact no credit was given to Moro's intelligence — which was at the very least superior to that of his captors. It would have been possible, without relinquishing the 'unyielding' attitude adopted, to continue arguing with him, either publicly by countering his suggestions — which were reasonable and by no means nonsensical — or privately by trying to discover any messages possibly, and probably concealed in his letters. Instead experts were employed to examine the Red Brigades' idiom — and it didn't require experts to find that it was miserably petrified, made of slogans, revolutionary clichés and gleanings from sociological and guerilla textbooks. Moreover it isn't of the slightest importance to discover whether or not the Red Brigades' Italian is a translation from another or other tongues. The Red Brigades' Italian is simply the Red Brigades' Italian. Theories can be construed about its various 'sources', but for the time being and for some time to come these must remain theories. And this passage from one of Moro's last letters might also help in their formulation: 'The Communists excuse their harshest rigours on such a principle, and to defend Communist solidarity' — a passage which hasn't as yet been accorded the significance, attention and analysis it deserves.

The principle Moro is referring to is that of not negotiating, of relentlessness. And it's natural he should assign it to the harshest Communist rigours which are now backing Christian Democracy — a Party whose lack of rigour he is in a position to know. But what does 'Communist solidarity' signify? Can he have been trying to hint at the possibility, if not at the certainty that there's a link between the Red Brigades and International Communism or some Communist country?

Inquiries into the existence of such a link (and not necessarily with Communism or Communist countries but with countries, regimes and governments which could and can find some advantage in the 'destabilization' of Italy) are among the tasks assigned to the Commission by Parliament, precisely under Items g) and h) of the Act. The answer, as regards links with foreign terrorist groups, can be given unhesitatingly: such links exist, though their frequency, consistency and relevance are not known precisely. But as to networks, conspiracies and international links beyond and above contacts, communications and mutual exchanges of terrorist groups, no definite answer is available. This is inevitable since in such matters definite answers only emerge in retrospect, from archives and for the historian's benefit.

It can be said that the names of certain foreign countries recur more or less frequently and persistently — and most frequently and pesistently those of Middle-Eastern countries, of Czechoslovakia, of Libya and, recently, of Bulgaria. But these are, according to those in charge whom the Commission interrogated, only 'rumours'. However one tends to suppose that it wasn't on 'rumours' alone that Onorevole Andreotti, then President of the Council, was replying when he referred in Senate at the session of 18 May to a country where Italian youths were trained for a given type of guerilla warfare and when, in reply to objections raised by Senator Bufalini, who thought he was alluding to the Soviet Union, he peremptorily asserted:

> Indeed, it emerged that certain terrorists accused of terrorist activities had been in Czechoslovakia. However, tens of thousands of people go to Czechoslovakia; nor could it be definitely proved that there was anything to distinguish them from ordinary tourists.

Obviously Onorevole Andreotti hadn't heard the 'rumour' that, among the tens of thousands of Italians who go to Czechoslovakia as 'tourists', Public Security had identified about six hundred who might be considered less touristic than the rest. And this 'rumour' derives from a report of SESIS [Executive Committee for Information and Security Services], certainly written after September 1979, which, with the help of further 'rumours' from SISMI [Military Information and Security Service], SISDE [Democratic Information and Security Service] and Carabinieri Headquarters asserts that:

> . . . at least 2000 Italians (according to surveys from various sources) between 1948 and the present have attended courses for extremist agitators in Czechoslovakia and other countries. Of these about 600 members are known to SISMI.

And as regards Czechoslovakia he added:

Predominantly in Milan and Rome there are members of the Czech secret service employed as contacts with various terrorist groups. These are detailed to provide an accurate documentation of candidates, all voluntary, which they transmit to the Czech Embassy whence it is in turn passed on to Prague. At this point those who are considered more notably dedicated, aggressive and militarily disposed are sent off and enrolled in actual paramilitary courses in Czechoslovakia or elsewhere and provided with false papers by their host country. Once they have completed their training the terrorists return to Italy with a substantial baggage of theoretical and practical guerilla warfare information which they are able to impart in their turn to other members of associated organizations.

And if this extract from the report, with all its details, is seen as 'rumour' then we can only say that the CESIS, SISMI, SISDE and the police force are only capable of obtaining 'rumours' and are no better than 'rumours' themselves, which, for the Italian tax-payer isn't very reassuring. Unless we agree with Doctor Lugaresi, head of SISMI:

As regards these International links, this is what I have to say: an important arms traffic exists which is difficult to stamp out because it's like the drugs traffic in that it's less a matter of politics than of trade. There are mutual exchanges of men who have a common purpose of 'destabilization'. There may be some kind of politico-strategic tendency. But it's up to our politicians to infer such things from the isolated scraps of information we supply daily.

Exactly. And it should be noted here that General Della Chiesa — who in his first deposition also tended to see as 'rumours' reports concerning the Red Brigades' links with foreign secret services and who considered Moretti to be the Red Brigades' 'top man' — when asked during his second deposition nearly two years later if he still held the same opinion, replied:

At present I have my doubts . . . Now I wonder (because today I'm outside the affray and for a little while I've been playing at observing on the basis of past experience) where are the files? Where is the original text (of the so-called Moro trial)? Was there no way of tracing the files, no repentant or reformed terrorist who could have referred to such things, or deplored their disappearance? . . . I believe there must be someone who appropriated all that . . . We should also take into consideration the trips abroad these people undertook. Moretti was always coming and going.

It's already something that he should have his doubts now — but a pity they only occurred once he was 'outside the affray'.

There's one detail which has to be mentioned as evidence of the imperceptible waning of any eagerness to find Aldo Moro. Immediately after the abduction, an International Security Committee was created which met on the 17th, 19th, 20th and 31st of March; once only in April on the 24th; and then on May the 3rd and 5th. But more significant still is the fact that the politico-technical operative group chaired by the Minister of the Interior and comprising Government executives, heads of the Police Force and of Information and Security Services, the Chief Constable of Rome and other Public Security officials, met daily until 31 March but after that only three times a week. Moreover, neither the minutes nor 'even records or deeds' of these later meetings 'can be traced'. And this group was expressly (and very sensibly) created for the purpose of studying the evidence and deciding, implementing and coordinating the operation.

Rome, 22 June 1982.

P.S. Deposited in June 1982 (since it had been initially established that reports should be deposited within that month), this report requires today that I make two amendments to the proofs owing to recent evidence acquired by the Commission:
1) The transit of the two printing presses found at the Triana Printing Office has finally been traced, as can be read in the Majority Report. Thus the fact that equipment discarded as scrap-iron by Government Offices finished up, in good working order, in the hands of the Red Brigades must be assigned to fate.
2) The statement ascribed to CESIS is deemed to have been made by SISMI. However, the impression remains when reading it that it derived from an organization that was part of SISMI.

Also of interest and available from
Granta Books

www.grantabooks.com

SICILIAN UNCLES
Leonardo Sciascia

'The master of sophisticated detective fiction remains
Leonardo Sciascia, whose novels are an extended investigation
into what it means to be Sicilian' *Guardian*

'In ordinary detective stories there is always a good deal of
disposable material, standard wrapping produced by the
simple necessity of having things happen somewhere. There is
nothing of the kind in Sciascia' Frank Kermode

A Sicilian uncle is a mentor, a patron, but a sinister and
treacherous one. This quartet of thriller novellas shows
illusions being lost and ideals betrayed amid war and
revolution. They are set at turning points of modern history:
the revolutions of 1848; the Spanish Civil War; the Allied
invasion of Sicily in 1943; and the death of Stalin ten years
later. Each story is full of vivid characters and is like a door
opening onto history. This is entertaining writing of a very
high order.

THE DAY OF THE OWL
Leonardo Sciascia

'Sciascia made out of his curious Sicilian experience a
literature that is not quite like anything else ever done by a
European' Gore Vidal

This short novel about the mafia is also a mesmerising
demonstration of how that organisation sustains itself. It is
both a beautifully written story and a brave act of
denunciation. A dark-suited man is shot as he runs for a bus
in the piazza of a small town. The investigating officer is a
man who believes in the values of a democratic and modern
society, and soon finds himself up against a wall of silence and
vested interests. The narrative moves on two levels: that of
the investigator, who reveals a chain of nasty crimes; and that
of the bystanders and watchers, of those complicit with secret
power, whose gossipy furtive conversations have only one
end: to stop the truth coming out.

THE WINE-DARK SEA
Leonardo Sciascia

'One of the major writers of the age' *Times Literary Supplement*

Here are some of Leonardo Sciascia's greatest stories, brief and haunting: the realist tradition at its best. In one tale a couple of men talk, cynically yet earnestly, about the etymology of the word 'mafia'. The reader comes to realize that he is eavesdropping on the musings of a mafia boss and his underling. In another story a group of peasants are taken on board ship and promised that they will be put ashore illegally at Trenton, New Jersey. After a long time at sea, their landfall is far from what they expected.